138404

HD
5854.55
U5
D38
1983

Davidson

Moonlighting

DATE DUE			
MAR 8 '89			
SEP 2 1 1994			

MOONLIGHTING

Also by Peter Davidson

EARN MONEY AT HOME!
Over 200 Ideas for Businesses
Requiring Little or No Capital

PETER DAVIDSON

MOONLIGHTING

A Complete Guide to Over 200 Exciting Part-time Jobs

McGRAW-HILL BOOK COMPANY

New York St. Louis San Francisco Bogotá Guatemala Hamburg Lisbon
Madrid Mexico Montreal Panama Paris San Juan São Paulo Tokyo Toronto

Copyright © 1983 by Peter Davidson
All rights reserved.
Printed in the United States of America.
Except as permitted under the Copyright Act of 1976,
no part of this publication may
be reproduced or distributed in any form
or by any means, or stored in a data
base or retrieval system, without the prior
written permission of the publisher.

23456789FGRFGR87654

ISBN 0-07-049607-2 {PBK}
     0-07-049601-3 {H.C.}

LIBRARY OF CONGRESS CATALOGING IN PUBLICATION DATA

Davidson, Peter, 1942–
Moonlighting: a complete guide to over 200 exciting part-time
jobs.
Includes index.
1. Supplementary employment—United States. 2. Part-time
employment—United States. I. Title.
HD5854.55.U5D38   1983   650.1′4   82–22884
ISBN 0-07-049607-2 (pbk.)
     0-07-049601-3 (H.C.)

Book design by Roberta Rezk

Dedicated to my sons, Les, Chris, Stuart, and Scott.
May they derive as much pleasure from Moonlighting *as I have.*

Peter Davidson

Contents

Introduction

SECRETARIES do it. Teachers do it. Factory workers do it. Even doctors and lawyers do it. Do what? *Moonlight*—that's what!

As the cost of living has soared, many people have found that the income from their regular job just isn't sufficient to allow them to live in the life-style they want. Therefore, millions of people have turned to working part-time, known as moonlighting, to supplement their income. It is estimated there are 5,000,000 moonlighters in America, and the number is growing! In addition to that, over 16,000,000 people work at part-time jobs as their sole employment.

Moonlighting has become a way of life for many families. The extra income might be the difference between taking a real vacation or staying home. It often provides extra money to trade cars regularly or to live in that dream house. It may be the difference between making ends meet and being hopelessly in debt.

In some cases, the moonlighting income has grown to be greater than that earned on the regular job. Many people have become so successful in their part-time moonlighting that they have quit their regular job and turned their moonlighting activity into a successful full-time career. In fact, moonlighting is a great way to try out a new career area before plunging into it on a full-time basis.

For some, the appeal of a second, part-time job, is not necessarily the money but the opportunity to work at an activity they truly enjoy. Many full-time jobs are very unful-filling. They are dead-end jobs that offer little satisfaction. The moonlighting activity, on the other hand, offers excitement, challenge, and a vehicle through which creativity can be expressed and explored.

You might ask: Are part-time jobs still available in an economy plagued with high unemployment and scores of people searching for a job? The answer is unmistakably yes! Even though unemployment is high, this does not mean that employers are not hiring. It often means, though, that employers are more selective and that the job hunter must be well organized and must use more job-hunting skill than ever before. In addition to moonlighting as an employee for someone else, of course, many possibilities exist to moonlight in some activity where you are self-employed or where you perform as an independent salesperson.

This book provides a thorough discussion of whether or not moonlighting is for you and offers an analysis of the legalities of moonlighting. Step-by-step procedures are offered on how to choose a moonlighting activity that meets your interests, abilities, and expectations. Different types of part-time jobs are analyzed, and the advantages and disadvantages of each type are explored. The section "Moonlighting Activities You Can Do" describes more than 200 part-time jobs in over 60 classifications. The section titled "How to Land a Part-time Job" provides practical information that can be followed to help you get the job you want. The sections "How to Establish Your Own Business or Service" and "How to Perform as a Salesperson" contain valuable information that will help you get started properly.

Most likely, many of the moonlighting jobs presented here will directly match your interests, abilities, and goals. In addition, many of these ideas will serve as a springboard for your imagination to develop your own unique way to earn money on a part-time basis. Even through *Moonlighting* is written with part-time jobs in mind, the information will also be of value for persons seeking full-time employment.

Well, the sun is setting in the west and daylight is growing dim; it's time to find out what this moonlighting is all about!

Part 1

Moonlighting—Is It for You?

Is MOONLIGHTING for you? This is one of those questions to which no universal answer exists. Many factors will affect your attitude and the attitude of others toward moonlighting. Without a doubt, some people would be only half a person if it were not for their moonlighting activities. Take, for instance, the factory worker who spends 40 hours per week performing the same activity over and over but who then occupies two exciting nights on the weekend as a local hero playing guitar in the hottest band in town. Or the secretary or clerical worker who toils in a pressure cooker of an office but who can relax by pursuing a second career as an interior decorator, window designer, retail clerk, or lifeguard. Or the lawyer, accountant, or business manager who is mentally exhausted at the end of the day but who finds a refreshing release in the field of sports officiating.

How about the person who has the most boring job but who can walk with head held high by being an auctioneer, locksmith, pawnshop operator, hypnotist, or piano tuner in his or her spare time. Or the person who simply doesn't earn a decent living at a regular job but who more than makes up for it as a part-time real estate salesperson, model, or dog groomer. Or the person whose ideas are generally bypassed at a job but who operates a vending-machine route, bait shop, or campground with the expertise, skill, and imagination of a top-notch manager. Or the person who loves his or her job, is satisfied with the income, and has no complaints but who looks upon moonlighting as a property manager, private investigator, promoter, or trapper as being extremely enjoyable, a hobby, or a great way to expand skills and interests.

Yes, there are a lot of situations where people find moonlighting to be attractive.

On the other side of the ledger, moonlighting is not for everyone. Some people don't have the strength to pursue one full-time career, fulfill family obligations, and still look for more work to do. For others, it is not worth giving up leisure time or hobbies to pursue a second job. For some, there is no legitimate reason to moonlight—their regular job is satisfying, challenging, and financially rewarding.

One reason that does not fit on this list, however, is lack of ability to land a part-time job or to develop one's own moonlighting activity. This is because there are literally dozens of opportunities for which virtually every person can qualify.

Let's make a methodical analysis of whether or not moonlighting is for you.

ANALYZING YOUR REASON
FOR MOONLIGHTING

Everyone who moonlights does so for a reason, which can be classified in one of two broad categories—monetary and nonmonetary.

By monetary, it is meant that a person moonlights primarily for the money. They either *need* the money for survival—to help pay the rent and utilities—or they *want* the money so they can lead a more comfortable and satisfying life-style.

By nonmonetary, it is meant that the prime motivation to

tackle a second, part-time job is the challenge, enjoyment, excitement, personal fulfillment, prestige, or similar driving force.

Certainly, many people decide to moonlight because of a combination of these two reasons, in varying proportions, rather than solely because of one or the other. It should be pointed out that both of these, the monetary and the nonmonetary, are legitimate, acceptable, and worthwhile reasons for securing a part-time job.

As the first step in determining whether you should become a moonlighter, you might answer this question: For what reason would I take a second, part-time job—monetary, nonmonetary, or both?

ANALYZING IF YOU HAVE THE TIME TO MOONLIGHT

Sure, you're busy—but just exactly what is it you're so busy doing? That's a tough question, because the day's activities aren't necessarily packaged in neat hour and half-hour blocks of time. Still, in order to determine if there are enough hours in your day or week to accommodate a part-time job, it is necessary to analyze how you are presently spending your time.

When we realize that there are 168 hours in the week and that perhaps 40 of them are consumed by your regular job and another 56 or so are used for sleeping, there are 72 unaccounted-for hours.

Undoubtedly, it would be interesting and revealing to record all of your activities for a week in fifteen-minute or half-hour segments. Since this is in itself quite time consuming, you may prefer to estimate your activities using Table 1 as a guideline. Take out a pencil and do it now.

Most likely, the results are quite surprising. Did you ever imagine that this was the way your time was being utilized? Then too, there is probably a substantial amount of time for

TABLE 1
Time Expended in a Week

Activity	Mon.	Tue.	Wed.	Thur.	Fri.	Sat.	Sun.	Week's Total
a. Work (regular job)								
b. Commuting to and from work								
c. Preparing meals								
d. Eating meals								
e. Household tasks								
f. Shopping								
g. Grooming and personal hygiene								
h. Time with spouse and/or children								
i. Television viewing								
j. Reading								
k. Hobbies and recreation								
l. Talking on telephone (for pleasure)								
m. Sleep								
n. Volunteer work for church, charity, etc.								
o. Other (specify)								
p. Other (specify)								
q. Total hours accounted for (add a through p)								
r. Total hours	24	24	24	24	24	24	24	168
s. Total hours unaccounted for (subtract q from r)								

which you were unable to account at all. This is not unusual, since nearly everyone has those 5-, 10-, or 20-minute time periods that just seem to slip away unnoticed. If they happen frequently, those short segments can add up in a hurry to lost hours. In fact, if a person wastes just 10 minutes 3 different times during the day, an incredible 10,950 minutes are lost each year —that's over 180 hours, or approximately four and a half workweeks!

So, is there time in your schedule to squeeze in a part-time job several hours per day, at night, or on the weekends? Perhaps you have that much time available in your schedule, or have enough unaccounted-for time that is not being used fruitfully, that you can easily say *yes* to that question.

On the other hand, if your time schedule appears to be full, you will need to decide if you can, or want to, rearrange activities and time allocations to make room for a part-time job. This decision will be based largely upon your perspective of life. That is, what you deem as being necessary or important will be your guide in determining how much time you should devote to any particular activity.

This requires identifying priorities, listing in order the things of greatest importance to you from highest interest to that of lowest significance. In doing so, you might ask yourself some questions such as the following: Is it worth it to me to give up two or three hours of television viewing per night to live in a more comfortable home? Am I willing to exchange those leisurely but unproductive Saturday afternoons for a real family vacation in the mountains or at the beach? Should I give up or cut down on bowling or golf in order to take a part-time job that might end up as a terrific full-time career?

In reality, most people probably have a good deal of unaccounted for time or poorly utilized time in their schedules. Therefore, it is often easy to find time to become a moonlighter by simply becoming better organized and by making better use of one's time. It is usually unnecessary to eliminate, or even drastically cut back, activities of great importance or strong interest. Efficient utilization of time—that is the key.

ANALYZING IF YOU HAVE THE STRENGTH TO MOONLIGHT

Perhaps the idea of moonlighting is intriguing and you have found the time in your schedule to do it. The next question is this: Do you have the strength, both physically and mentally, to handle a part-time job? The answer to this is easy: some people do and some do not.

Your own answer to whether or not you have the strength to be a moonlighter will be easy for you to find. Mostly, it will rest within your *attitude* toward your part-time job. If you want to moonlight, if you are excited about it, if you find it challenging and rewarding, and if you are convinced it is worth whatever you are trading in terms of leisure or television-viewing time, don't worry about it, you *will* have the strength. In fact, if you possess this type of positive attitude, you will most likely find that your moonlighting activity will leave you refreshed and exhilarated, rather than drained.

On the other hand, if you would rather be someplace else, doing something other than moonlighting, or if you find it to be a chore or obligation, your part-time job will probably sap both your physical and mental strength.

This does not necessarily mean that you must abandon the idea of moonlighting. What it does indicate, though, is that you should find a different moonlighting activity—one that is interesting, challenging, and exciting. The resultant change in your attitude, from negative to positive, will bring with it a remarkable increase in physical strength and mental stamina.

There are, of course, situations where people should not even consider tackling a part-time job in addition to a regular job and other activities. For instance, if you spend 70 hours per week at your regular job, that's enough, and then some. Or if you are actually frail or have a physical health problem or nervous condition, your time might be better spent relaxing and conserving your energies.

In summary, it might be said that the person of average physical and mental health easily has the strength to work in the neighborhood of 60 to 65 hours per week without any ill effects whatsoever. In fact, until a fairly recent point in history, virtually *everyone* worked 60 hours or more per week. A workweek of that length is still commonplace among business managers and self-made millionaires—people who put in their time to get to the top and who are doing what it takes to stay there.

ANALYZING YOUR PRESENT EMPLOYER'S ATTITUDE

Employer's attitudes toward moonlighting vary from one end of the spectrum to the other. Some are afraid that the moonlighting will be overdone, to the employer's detriment. Others are intimidated by it, being fearful that the moonlighter may become too independent or perhaps (horrors!) pass them by in personal earnings. Still others are somewhat embarrassed by it because it doesn't "look right" in the community. And there are those who feel degraded by it, since it appears to others that their employees need to work at two jobs to earn a decent living.

On the other hand, some employers almost *expect* their employees to moonlight to keep current in their field or to enhance the employer's reputation and prestige. Sometimes, highly regarded employees can afford to stay in their employ only because they supplement their earnings by moonlighting.

Some secure and farsighted managers recognize and admire a moonlighter for what he or she often truly is—a person with drive, ambition, goals, and determination, who wants to get ahead in life.

Then too, there are employers who feel that moonlighting is acceptable in some situations but not in others.

The Legalities of Moonlighting

Ordinarily, the questions asked about the legalities of moonlighting are of the following nature: Can my present employer prohibit me from taking a part-time job elsewhere? If I currently have a part-time job, can my regular employer make me quit? Are some types of jobs acceptable for me to work at part-time, in my employer's eyes, while others may not be?

The answers to these questions depend upon the circumstances. A primary factor, though, is whether the topic of moonlighting is addressed in your employment contract with your regular employer. If this contract says you may, or may not, work at an outside part-time job, that settles it. Do as the contract says.

If the contract prohibits moonlighting and you do it anyway, you have breached your contract and are subject to reprimand or dismissal. If your contract prohibits moonlighting and you disagree with these terms, your only redress is to try to negotiate a new contract with your employer, changing those terms.

Rarely does a controversy arise when a contract specifically states whether you may or may not moonlight. You either can or you can't, and that's it. Where the controversies ordinarily arise is when the employer is silent on the topic of moonlighting—as many of them are. There is no policy that says you can moonlight, but then, there is no policy that says you can't either.

In general, if the contract does not specifically state or imply that you cannot moonlight, your employer probably cannot rightfully prohibit you from doing so. There are some guidelines that must be followed though. One is that your part-time job must not create a *conflict of interest* with your primary, regular job. This means you cannot work for your employer's competitors, directly or indirectly compete with your employer, or injure or endanger your employer's business in any way. For example, if you work full-time for the Washington Bank, it would undoubtedly be a conflict of interest to moonlight for the rival Franklin Bank. In another example, if you are employed by Adams Plumbing Company as a plumber, it would be a conflict of interest to operate your own plumbing business part-time on the weekends in the same trade area.

Another situation where your moonlighting activity will cause problems is if it interferes in any way with your ability to do your job for your regular employer. An example would be if you are so tired from working half the night at your part-time job that you are ineffective at your regular position. Another is if you do not devote your full attention to your employer's business during the regular workday but instead pursue some of your moonlighting interests. Another would be if your moonlighting activity is grossly inconsistent with or contrary to your regular job, like a full-time minister moonlighting as a bartender.

In any of these situations, the employer would most likely be justified in requiring you to abandon your moonlighting activities or in discharging you.

How about the situation, however, where your moonlighting activity in no way conflicts with your employer's business, and where you in no way allow it to interfere with the performance of your duties for you regular employer? Can that employer prohibit you from moonlighting? This is a common question, and often a sticky one, although the answer is quite clear and easily arrived at. The answer is no, the employer should not be able to stop you from moonlighting, unless there is a clause to that effect in your contract. Next time the contract is negotiated, of course, the employer may attempt to introduce a clause prohibiting moonlighting.

The preceding are general guidelines. Since every situation can have its own peculiarities and quirks, it is suggested that you consult an attorney for advice if there is doubt as to your situation.

Of course, another solution is to openly discuss your intended moonlighting plans with your employer before you start your second job. Most employers like to be informed firsthand of any moves made by employees that might be potentially jolting or embarrassing. If you assure your employer that your moonlighting activities will not create a conflict or become too consuming of your time and energies, you might receive your employer's blessing and thwart any potential problems before they begin. On the other hand, informing your employer of your intentions to moonlight may have the same effect as waving a red flag in front of a raging bull. You may be better off leaving well enough alone and quietly and discreetly going about your business.

In general, it might be stated that if you pursue your moonlighting activities in a low-profile manner, without drawing undue attention, you will probably be subjected to very little or no criticism or scrutiny from your employer. You will be able to happily pursue your interests without interference.

It is a good idea when interviewing for a new job to sound out your prospective employer on attitudes toward moonlighting. Often, the one chance that you will have to negotiate a mutually acceptable understanding on your moonlighting activities occurs before you are hired. To avoid any future misinterpretation, it will be beneficial to include this agreement in your written employment contract.

Part 2

Choosing the Right Moonlighting Activity

LET'S assume you have determined that you have the time and strength to moonlight and have an interest in doing so. Now, you must find an acceptable part-time activity. You can approach this haphazardly, taking whatever happens to come along, or you can devote some time and effort to carefully selecting a compatible moonlighting activity.

Certainly, the second procedure is recommended. As long as you're going to work at a part-time job, it may as well be something that you will find interesting and enjoyable and which will provide a satisfactory amount of income.

The process of selecting an acceptable moonlighting activity involves an analysis of your personal goals, interests, abilities, financial needs, financial goals, and available time. In addition, good timing is necessary in selecting an activity that is currently popular or that has long-lasting appeal and potential.

ANALYZING YOUR PERSONAL GOALS

What do you want out of life? Where do you want to be occupationally, financially, and personally a month, 6 months, a year, 5 years, 10 years, or 20 years from now? Have you ever really given it serious thought? Well, if you haven't, it is now time to do so.

Start by taking out pencil and paper and actually writing down what you would like to accomplish at various time intervals in your future, for perhaps the next 5, 10, or 15 years. Since major achievements are ordinarily accomplished slowly over a period of time, break any major or long-term goals into smaller or short-term segments.

Now that you have identified *what* you want to accomplish, you must decide *how* you will do it, for things do not ordinarily just happen by themselves—you must *make* them happen. It is therefore necessary to develop a plan for reaching the goals you have set. This plan should consist of a series of steps, small steps, you will take to inch yourself along steadily until you reach your goals.

Most likely, your pursuit of a part-time job will play an integral role in the establishment and achievement of your goals. For many people, it is moonlighting activity that provides the extra income or challenge that makes planning for the future and the establishment of goals worthwhile and realistic.

ANALYZING YOUR INTERESTS AND ABILITIES

If you match your moonlighting activity to an area where you have interest and ability, it will be a marriage that will yield great satisfaction and that enhances your prospects of achieving success.

Using your pencil and paper, make a list of absolutely *everything* that is of interest to you or that you like to do. Include hobbies, volunteer activities, household tasks, recreational interests, leisure activities, and, yes, even dreams and fantasies.

An analysis of your abilities can be undertaken in the same way. Write down every skill, knowledge, and ability you possess. Include things for which you have received formal training and certification as well as those things that you have learned on your own through a hobby, raising a family, by doing volunteer work, or by reading and self study. Don't overlook positive physical attributes, intelligence, athletic prowess, musical ability, or good business sense. Include intangibles like being well organized, efficient, alert, conscientious, dependable, and prompt.

After preparing your lists of interests and abilities, you should analyze them. Pinpoint your strongest interests and your most salable abilities. As you read through the "Moonlighting Activities You Can Do" section, keep your interests and abilities foremost in mind. Undoubtedly, there will be several activities for which you are perfectly suited.

In addition, there will most likely be some moonlighting activities that sound appealing but for which you do not appear to have a suitable background or proper training. In this situation, a thorough study of the job entry requirements, necessary skills, and methods of obtaining training should be undertaken. This analysis should be coupled with a review of your long-term goals. In many cases, it may be well worth embarking on a training program to gain the abilities necessary to enter an attractive employment area.

ANALYZING YOUR FINANCIAL NEEDS AND GOALS

There are three questions that you might ask yourself at this point: (1) How much money do I *need* to earn at a part-time job to provide me with the additional income I require? (2) How much money do I *want* to earn as a moonlighter? (3) How much money is it *possible* to earn at a part-time job?

The answer to the first question, how much money you need, can be calculated by making a careful study of the dollar cost of that dream vacation, new car, or other planned expenditures for which your moonlighting income will be used.

When calculating the amount of income you want to earn,

the goals that you have established should be your guide. You will find the amount by answering this question: What is it that you want to do, and how much money is required to do it?

The income potential of each type of moonlighting activity you are considering should be carefully analyzed and compared with your financial needs and wants. With some types of part-time jobs, the normal income level is at or about the minimum wage rate. With others, it is readily possible to earn thousands of dollars per month. In some cases, for instance if you are an employee, you may be assured of receiving a weekly or monthly paycheck of a certain amount. In other cases, for example if you become involved in sales or operate your own business or service, there may be no assured income at all, and your pay periods may be very sporadic.

In making your projections of the amount of income each type of moonlighting activity can yield, it is important that the net earnings from each be compared. This is the amount of real earnings after deducting various costs for transportation, clothing, equipment, supplies, baby-sitting fees, or any other expenditures incurred because of your moonlighting activity.

ANALYZING YOUR AVAILABLE TIME

The amount of time and the type of time you have available to devote to your moonlighting activity, as previously calculated, should be considered as you study each type of opportunity available to you.

Some part-time jobs call for a regular schedule of a certain number of hours per day, at the same time every day, week after week. With others, there is no set schedule at all—you work when you want to or whenever you can land a client who needs your assistance. In some cases, the work exists steadily year round, while other jobs are seasonal.

If you have only a few hours per week that can be devoted to a part-time job, you undoubtedly can find a moonlighting activity that will be suitable. On the other hand, there are many "part-time jobs" that can occupy 40, 50, or 60 hours per week if you want them to or if you will let them. Of course, there are many moonlighting opportunities that occupy a time somewhere between these two extremes.

Often, the same moonlighting activity can be pursued for either a few hours or for many hours per week or per month, depending upon how you approach it.

ANALYZING YOUR TIMING

The term *timing* often crops up when an analysis is made of why someone was successful at a particular venture when others had failed. As it pertains to moonlighting, timing is picking an activity that is popular now, that will remain so in the future, and that holds good promise for continued success.

Good timing is usually not an accident; ordinarily it is based upon study and analysis. The general state of the nation's economy, the local economic situation, trends that are starting to evolve, and changes in people's interests are all factors that should be considered. Often, the topics of books on the best-seller lists and those that command time in the news media and on various talk-show programs will give you a clue to areas in which people have an interest.

One of the real advantages of moonlighting is that you probably will not have the amount of money, time, or educational training invested in a part-time job that you would in a full-time career area. Therefore, it is often easier to move from one moonlighting area to another if it appears that the timing is right to do so.

Part 3

Types of Moonlighting Activities

A PART-TIME JOB can be pursued in a number of different ways. Primarily, you can either work for someone else or operate your own business or service. A third possibility is to perform as a salesperson, which combines features of working for someone else and working for yourself. This section explores characteristics of moonlighting in each way and discusses advantages and disadvantages of each.

WORKING FOR SOMEONE ELSE

Nearly every activity presented in *Moonlighting* can be undertaken by working for someone else. It is often the simplest, most direct, and most worry-free way to earn money on a part-time basis.

Skills and Abilities Needed

To become successful in working for someone else, two types of skills and abilities are needed—*technical* and *personal*.

Technical skill refers to the specific knowledge needed to do the job, such as the ability to type, prepare tax forms, repair locks, tune pianos, weld, or install carpet. In some cases, a certain amount of training and licensing or certification may be necessary as a prerequisite to securing the position. In others, no special skills are required or they are learned on the job.

Personal skill refers to those personal qualities that are necessary for success on any job, like being cooperative, conscientious, honest, dependable, prompt, hard working, and willing to follow directions.

Advantages

A primary advantage of working for someone else is that little or no investment is ordinarily required. Another is that the ultimate responsibility for major decisions and for any financial losses rests with someone else—the person or company for whom you work. In addition, the amount of skill and ability needed by you is limited to the tasks you perform; you do not need to know everything about running the entire operation.

Another advantage is that working for someone else can be an ideal learning experience before establishing your own business or service. Also, it is easy to change jobs or to quit altogether by simply giving notice of your intentions.

Disadvantages

A disadvantage of working for someone else is that you do not receive the full financial rewards or recognition that result from your ideas and hard work. Another is that the pay level and earnings potential may be limited. Also, opportunities for advancement may be restricted and it may be difficult to develop your part-time job into a well-paying full-time career.

OPERATING YOUR OWN BUSINESS OR SERVICE

The goal of many people is to be their own boss—perhaps you are one of them. True, the risks are often greater than those involved in working for someone else, but since risk and potential rewards go hand in hand, the possible returns are also greater. If you are of venturesome spirit and have confidence in your own skills and abilities, operating your own business or service may be the ideal way to moonlight.

Skills and Abilities Needed

The same types of technical and personal skills that are necessary to successfully work for someone else are also required to be successful in working for yourself. The technical skills include the knowledge to perform the activities involved in your particular type of business or service. The personal skills involve those qualities of putting forth a conscientious, dedicated effort, and possessing good human relations abilities.

In addition, a third type of skill is necessary. This involves the ability to organize and manage your activities, and possibly those of others as well. This skill should not be taken lightly, for it is this area, management, that ordinarily causes one operation to be a howling success while another is a dismal flop.

In essence, management amounts to making decisions. Good managers make good decisions at the right time. Poor managers make poor decisions or, perhaps worse yet, fail to make decisions at all.

Advantages

The opportunity to express and explore your own ideas and to do things exactly as you want is among the primary advantages of operating your own business or service. The challenge and excitement of running your own operation also ranks high on the list. Then too, being able to accept full responsibility for the operation's success or failure is often appealing.

Another big advantage is that you will receive all the profits generated by your ideas and efforts. Likewise, the potential exists to develop the part-time business or service into a full-time career that provides an outstanding income and life-style.

Disadvantages

Some of the factors looked upon as being advantages of operating your own business or service can also become a disadvantage. One of these is that a tremendous amount of responsibility rests upon the shoulders of the owner-operator. Another is that a wide range of skills and abilities are often required, and it is difficult for any one person to possess them all. Still another factor is that it is often more difficult to start one's own operation than to simply secure a job working for someone else.

Also, if the operation fails, a substantial financial loss might be suffered. Then too, if it becomes necessary or advisable to terminate the operation, it may be time consuming and costly to wind up the affairs.

It should be mentioned that many of these potential disadvantages can be eliminated through careful planning and by seeking the advice of persons who are knowledgeable in an area where assistance is needed.

PERFORMING AS A SALESPERSON

Many interesting and lucrative moonlighting opportunities exist in the sales field, and salesmanship is also an integral part of many other types of occupations.

This discussion pertains to the *independent salesperson*—that is, someone who sells under a company supervisor's general direction and control but who has a great deal of freedom and flexibility in how his or her sales activities and time schedule are handled. Those who sell real estate, life insurance, or products like vacuum cleaners, sewing machines, advertising specialties, cutlery, or cosmetics to consumers in their homes or to businesses fall within this category.

As an independent salesperson, you ordinarily can work when you like and use whatever sales techniques you want, as long as you do not violate company policies. Earnings are usually calculated on a commission basis, whereby you receive a percentage of sales made, or according to another arrangement that is directly related to your volume of sales. Ordinarily, independent salespersons pay all, or most, of their own sales-related expenses.

Although being a retail salesclerk is not specifically included in this discussion, most of the skills and abilities required to be a successful independent salesperson also apply. The job of retail salesclerk, however, is essentially like working for someone else as an employee.

Skills and Abilities Needed

All salespeople need to possess two basic types of skills and abilities—these are *product knowledge* and the *ability to sell.*

As the term implies, product knowledge refers to knowing and understanding your product. In general, you should understand how the product or service is used, who can best use it, and what benefits it will provide for your prospective customers.

The ability to sell involves many aspects, such as prospecting for customers, making a professional sales presentation, answering objections, closing the sale, and handling all details involved in the sale of your product or service. Essentially, sales ability amounts to recognizing a prospect's needs and identifying how your product or service will satisfy those needs.

Salespeople must possess a friendly nature and be aggressive yet not overbearing or high pressure. Mental agility is required to keep pace with the prospect and to find solutions to the prospect's problems. Perseverance is also necessary, since many prospects will buy, but not necessarily the first time they are asked. Then too, maturity and the ability to withstand occasional disappointments are important, since not every hard-fought presentation will result in a sale.

Some people are reluctant to enter the sales profession because they are fearful that they do not possess satisfactory speaking abilities. This is usually a gross misconception. Speaking ability is necessary, yes, but you do not need to be a great orator. Since you are always talking about a topic that you thoroughly understand—your product or service—and usually talk to only one or two people at a time, selling actually amounts to carrying on a conversation rather than making a speech, giving a lecture, or teaching a class of students.

In addition, you must be a highly-motivated self-starter capable of organizing your time and directing your activities toward fruitful activities. You must also be assertive, since it is often necessary to seek out customers.

In order to be successful in the sales field, you should possess a real desire to be of service to your customers, and their welfare must always be foremost in all your dealings.

Advantages

A major advantage of being a salesperson is that your earnings will be in direct relationship to the amount and quality of effort you put forth. Also, there is often the opportunity to supplement your income by winning company-sponsored sales contests and bonus awards. In addition, there is much flexibility in being able to work when and how you want. Also, there is often little, if any, cash investment required to get started. In many respects, you are your own boss operating your own business without the usual risks involved in business ownership.

The great feeling of accomplishment that comes from convincing a customer to buy and from knowing that you have been of service to your customers should not be overlooked as an advantage of being a salesperson. Furthermore, it is very interesting work, where no two transactions are handled in exactly the same way.

Disadvantages

A disadvantage of being a salesperson is that there is usually no guaranteed income—if you don't sell, you earn nothing, even though you have expended a great deal of time and effort. Another is that there is often stiff competition, with many other salespeople vying for your customers' business.

Still another is that it can be discouraging work because, on occasion, you will spend a great deal of time working with a customer, only to have your high hopes shattered when the prospect refuses to buy or buys from someone else.

Part 4

Moonlighting Activities You Can Do

THE MOONLIGHTING activities described in this section cover a wide range, from those that require little or no previous training or background to others for which special knowledge, certification, or licensing is necessary. Some involve providing a service, while others deal in the sale of a product. Little or no investment is required to enter most areas, but there are several where a substantial cash outlay is necessary.

Most of the activities can be either operated on your own or pursued by working for someone else. With some opportunities, you would work regularly scheduled hours, but most can be pursued on a flexible time schedule. Some activities provide a steady, guaranteed income, while the income from others is dependent upon how hard and how well you work. All of them can be entered on a part-time basis and hold the potential to be developed into a full-time career.

Over 200 moonlighting opportunities are described in over 60 categories. No doubt, many of them will match your interests, abilities, available time, income requirements, and future goals. Even though many may be appealing, your objective should be to select only one—the *one* that is ideal for you.

Advertising Specialty Sales

L ET'S CONDUCT a little survey. Take a good look at the pens, pencils, and matchbooks stashed in your drawers, and at your nearest calendar. Is there any printing on them? Most likely there is, and in many cases it is the name of some bank, restaurant, insurance agency, or other business. You received these items free because they constitute a form of advertising for whoever gave them to you. These items are called *advertising specialties* or *novelties*.

Where do these organizations get their advertising specialties? Well, most of them are purchased directly from someone involved in *advertising specialty sales*. This salesperson is affiliated with a manufacturer or distributor of these popular products.

The potential clients for advertising specialty products are easy to define—*everyone*. Sales are made to small businesses, to the nation's largest companies, and to everyone and everything in between. Look at the possibilities: banners, pens, pencils, jackets, and notebooks for schools and colleges; calendars, memo pads, and matchbooks for real estate agencies, nightclubs, and manufacturers; jackets, shirts, and caps for company-sponsored bowling and softball teams; and balloons and trinkets for open houses and grand openings. Other potential clients that should not be overlooked include service organizations and clubs, churches, unions, athletic teams, and even individuals.

In addition to selling smaller items, many advertising specialty salespeople service the huge market for business premiums and business gifts. These include almost any product imaginable that merchants give away to customers in contests or use as premiums for customers having made purchases of a certain value. Examples would be camping gear, sportswear, or household articles.

People who sell advertising specialties display their products in catalogs and frequently offer free samples. Orders are taken and submitted to the salesperson's company, and the company then ships the products to the buyer.

Most advertising specialty companies require minimum orders, of say $50, to be submitted. Potential exists, of course, to land a big account. Some companies, in fact, buy over a million dollars of advertising specialties per year!

Salespeople are paid on a commission basis. The commission rate varies widely with type of item sold and size of order. The range is generally from 10 to 25 percent of the sales amount. For example, if a $500 order is submitted and the commission rate is 20 percent, $100 is earned. Great potential exists to build repeat customers who will buy products from you year after year. Therefore, the longer you are at it, the easier your job becomes and the more your income grows.

Some advertising specialty companies assign exclusive territories to their salespeople. Others allow their salespeople to sell anywhere in the country. In any case, the salesperson works for only one company rather than representing several.

If selling advertising specialties on a part-time basis sounds exciting to you, that is with good reason—it *is* exciting. It can be a great way to earn that extra money you want by selling a lot of fun products and enjoying yourself at the same time.

The advertising specialties capital of the world is Newton, Iowa. The world's largest advertising specialties company, the Vernon Company, and another industry biggie, the Newton Manufacturing Company, are both located there. Addresses of these companies and others in the field, and the Specialty Advertising Association, International, are listed below. You may wish to contact one of them to get started selling the pens, pencils, calendars, whistles, and everything else for which everyone in the world is a potential client.

The Vernon Company
Newton, IA 50208

Newton Manufacturing Company
Newton, IA 50208

Jack Nadel & Associates
9950 Jefferson
Culver City, CA 90230

K-Promotions
3825 West Greentree Road
Milwaukee, WI 53200

Specialty Advertising Association, International
1404 Walnut Hill Lane
Irving, TX 75060

Animal-Related Occupations

ARE YOU an animal lover? If so, there are numerous
moonlighting opportunities available for you to consider in *an-imal-related occupations*. Some of these require an investment in
equipment, supplies, facilities, and pet stock, while others re-
quire little cash to get started. The one requirement common to
all of them is a genuine understanding of and love for animals.
Let's explore several categories.

Pet Training: As a pet trainer, you will teach pets obedience,
manners, routines, and tricks or stunts. The obvious pets that
come to mind are dogs and cats, but others like horses, birds,
and parrots are also worth considering.

To be a successful pet trainer, you must first understand the
pet's characteristics. This includes the age at which pets learn
best, the type of activities they can be expected to learn, and
their retention span.

The basic technique used in teaching all pets is repetition.
Perform the same activity over and over with the pet until this

behavior pattern is learned and becomes second nature. Reward the pet for successful completion of the task and reinforce the behavior pattern by lavishing praise and offering food.

Individual or group lessons can be offered, and the pet's owner may or may not be included in the training sessions. For best and most long-lasting results, however, the owner should be trained at least well enough to conduct practice sessions. Animals, like people, tend to forget what has been learned if it is not put to regular use.

Pet training can be learned by studying books; talking to other pet trainers, pet shop operators, or veterinarians, and most importantly, by experimentation and practice. Licensing is not required in many states. However, it will be worthwhile to receive certification if it is available, even if not required.

Set your rates by the hour or establish a flat amount for a training program consisting of several sessions. You might offer several different levels or types of instruction, and you can also offer periodic refresher courses and seminars.

Pet Boarding: A prime requirement to operate a pet boarding operation is that you must have a suitable location, one with sufficient available space and facilities. Exactly what is needed will vary with the types of pets you accept for boarding, but individual enclosures that are clean, free of disease, well ventilated, and escape-proof are musts.

Develop policies pertaining to types and sizes of pets you will accommodate. Establish regular business hours when pets can be deposited and picked up. You might offer a pickup and delivery service to make your offerings more attractive and to earn additional income.

Require owners to sign an agreement, releasing you from liability if their pets escape or become ill or die through no fault of yours. Also, get written permission to seek veterinary care if the pet requires attention. You will probably be required to have a license.

Charge a daily boarding fee that is in line with that charged by competitors in the area. You might also offer a weekly rate for those owners who will have extended absences. If extraordinary care is required or if special services like grooming are provided, charge an extra fee.

Pet Grooming: As a pet groomer, you will trim, cut, and perhaps shampoo a pet's coat. You will also trim and polish claws and nails. This skill can be learned by attending a grooming school or by working with an experienced groomer. Courses offered by grooming schools often last several weeks or months on a one- or two-nights-per-week basis.

Once you have learned your trade and have assembled a few basic pieces of equipment and supplies, you are ready to start this profitable business. A relatively small investment is required in professional clippers, scissors, brushes, combs, and miscellaneous items.

Rates can be set at a flat amount for a certain size or type of pet. Often, the charge for grooming dogs is set at a rate per inch, measuring from the ground to the dog's shoulder. Regardless of the method, a skilled pet groomer can earn an enviable hourly income, perhaps 3 to 6 times the minimum wage rate. Additional fees are often assessed if the pet's coat is extraordinarily matted, if extra time and skill is required for a show-quality pet, or if shampooing is requested.

An attractive feature of pet grooming as a moonlighting activity is that you will work by appointment, with clients bringing the pets to you and later picking them up.

Pet Breeding: People generally buy animals such as cats or dogs for one of two reasons—to have a family pet or to enter in show competition. Many people, of course, buy show-quality animals for pets. As a pet breeder, you can raise and sell either kind, but since the show-quality pets are far more expensive, your best profit potential ordinarily exists there.

Establish your pet breeding business by purchasing one or

more females. You can buy your own males, or you can use a stud service. Ideally, the breeding stock should be registered to make the offspring more readily salable and to command higher prices.

You can sell the pets directly to individuals or pet shops in your local area, or you can advertise in nationally circulated pet magazines. Air freight can safely be used to ship pets virtually anywhere.

First-rate facilities that are clean, disease-free, heated, and air-conditioned should be established for your pet breeding business. This, along with the initial cost for breeding stock, food, and medical attention, can require a fairly substantial investment. The income potential can be great, however, since high-quality registered pets often bring significant amounts, perhaps several hundred dollars each.

Raising smaller pets, like birds, fish, parrots, and rabbits, should also be considered for sale to individuals and to pet shops in your area.

Licensing requirements vary from state to state for each of these animal-related occupations. Often, no license or permit is required to become a pet trainer or groomer. Usually, licensing is required to operate a boarding kennel or to become a pet breeder. Check with your State Department of Agriculture to determine specific requirements. If you become a commercial pet breeder, a federal license may be necessary from the U.S. Department of Agriculture. Ordinarily, these licenses are easy to obtain. If a license is required, a state inspector may periodically visit your facilities to see that they are clean and disease-free and that the animals are receiving satisfactory treatment.

These animal-related occupations, particularly pet training and pet grooming, can be operated from your home if you have sufficient space and facilities and if local zoning regulations allow. Some of these activities, like pet breeding or operating a boarding kennel, may require a good deal of space and specialized facilities. Therefore, a rural or business location may be necessary.

You might moonlight at one of these animal-related occupations or enter several of them. In any case, your success will largely depend upon your attitude toward the animals and the loving care that you give them. Besides your own promotional activities, word of mouth from one satisfied animal lover to another will help build a steady and lasting clientele.

Announcer

I<small>F YOU</small> have been referred to as being silver tongued, your extraordinary speaking abilities can be put to work as an *announcer*.

Many possibilities exist to earn money part-time as an announcer, such as hosting local radio programs on sports, music, art, gardening, hobbies, and many other topics, or as a disc jockey. If your local radio station serves several area communities, you might become a correspondent, producing your own local news program via telephone hookup. Similar possibilities exist for programs of special interest for your local television station.

Other opportunities for plying your talents include being an announcer or emcee at banquets, fashion shows, contests, sporting events, home shows, beauty pageants, and other special events. You might also consider making radio commercials, particularly if you are adept at voice impersonations. Contact area radio stations, advertising agencies, and professional recording studios to inquire about this possibility.

What about licensing—isn't a license required to be an announcer on a radio or television program? The answer to this is no. Recent changes in Federal Communications Commission

(FCC) regulations now provide that no license is required to be an announcer or disc jockey on the radio or to be a television announcer. If you go beyond announcing and actually operate the control panel and take transmitter readings, you will need a *restricted permit*. This is obtained by simply filling out a card and submitting it to the FCC; no training, testing, or even fees are required to obtain it.

The primary skill that you need to be an announcer, whether it be on radio, television, or for some event, is the ability to speak. Your voice must be pleasant sounding and you must be able to speak fluently without stammering or ummming and ahhhing. You will need to be quick-witted so you can react to impromptu situations. A cool head is required, and you must be able to "think on your feet."

Although no special training is required to become an announcer, you may find it helpful. Courses in speech and drama from a local college are ideal; or you might enroll in a 9- or 12-month program at a broadcast institute.

Virtually no investment, except that which you might spend for training, is required to become an announcer. Since you are providing a personal service, little equipment, material, or supplies are needed.

If you have an idea for a special-interest program or want to be a sportscaster or disc jockey for your local radio station, develop your format, prepare a sample tape on a tape recorder, and approach the station manager. If you want to enter television announcing, proceed similarly.

If you want to specialize in fashion shows, contact local clothiers or clothing manufacturers. If banquets, trade shows, and the like are of interest to you, contact your Chamber of Commerce, convention centers, area trade associations, and large businesses that hold conventions and special events. After you have successfully demonstrated your ability at a few events, you will become more and more in demand.

As a part-time announcer on a radio or television program,

you will be paid an hourly wage, monthly salary, or flat rate per show, which can vary widely, from perhaps 2 to 10 times or more the minimum wage rate. If you work trade shows and other special events, you will most likely be paid a contracted fee per event, which might range from a mere honorarium to several hundred dollars. Your earnings will be determined largely by the type of announcing you perform, your ability, and your popularity.

In addition to the personal satisfaction and earnings received from being an announcer, a certain degree of celebrity status will be accorded to you. This makes announcing one of the most exciting of all moonlighting activities.

If you are intrigued by the broadcast area but are not enthused about becoming an announcer, you might moonlight as a *radio or television station engineer*. Here, you would operate transmitter equipment, take transmitter readings, and work with other behind-the-scenes technology.

Previously, the FCC required a third-, second-, or first-class license in order for a person to operate transmittal equipment. Recently, however, FCC regulations have been relaxed and these three classes have been replaced with a single designation, a *general radio telephone license*. The FCC can be contacted at the following address for more information on their regulations and requirements: Federal Communications Commission, 1919 M Street N.W., Washington, DC 20554.

Auctioneer

"WELL-ALRIGHT-NOW, I-got-59-dollars, would-you-give-60, do-you-want-'em-at-a-60, say-that-60, le'-me-hear-that-60-dollars, going-once, going-twice. . . ." If you raised your hand, nodded, or even winked convincingly, you have just bought yourself a magnificent, solid brass unicorn—for $60 at an auction! If you like this type of excitement and frenzied action, perhaps you should consider moonlighting as an *auctioneer*.

Auctioneers sell a variety of items, including household goods, real estate, automobiles, livestock, coins, art, farm equipment, and just about anything else.

The auctioneer's chant is the most identifiable characteristic of the auctioneer. It is true that mastering the chant is a big part of entering this profession, but other skills are necessary as well. Those connected with conduct of the sale include having a powerful and pleasant-sounding voice and displaying a pleasing, jovial, and even humorous personality. Good judgment and good timing are also necessary to pace the sale properly so that the highest prices are obtained but so that the sale does not drag on at a snail's pace.

The behind-the-scenes activities performed by an auctioneer are fully as important as those which auction-goers see. These include appraising goods, handling advertising, recommending the most appropriate time for the auction, and marking and displaying the goods. In other words, to become a successful auctioneer, a person must combine speaking and salesmanship skills with a strong business background.

Training to become an auctioneer can be obtained in a number of ways. The fastest of these is to attend an auctioneering school. There are several dozen of these scattered throughout the country, and most of them offer a concentrated program of two weeks or so in length. A partial list of these schools can be obtained by contacting the National Auctioneer's Association, 135 Lakewood Drive, Lincoln, NE 68510, or by consulting a trade school directory at your public library. A slower but also effective way to learn auctioneering is to work with an active auctioneer as an apprentice.

Licensing procedures to become an auctioneer vary widely from state to state, and counties and cities within each state may also have special requirements. Some states require that an exam be taken, while others grant a license upon payment of a fee only. In general, it is quite easy to meet licensing requirements to become an auctioneer. Contact the Board of Auctioneering in your state capital for specific information. In most states, a real estate license is also necessary to sell real property at an auction.

Auctioneers are ordinarily paid on a commission basis, receiving a percent of the total sales price for goods at the auction. The rate varies with the type of goods and from auctioneer to auctioneer because of their reputation and experience. The earnings from a small sale may be minimal, but several thousand dollars might be earned from a large sale or from the sale of real estate. It is not uncommon for a successful full-time auctioneer to have annual earnings similar to that of lawyers, accountants, or real estate brokers. Even part-time auctioneers can earn thousands of dollars per year. Most auctioneers are actually part-timers, since they couple this activity with one or two other business interests.

Because many auctions are conducted on evenings and weekends, the time schedule can be ideal for many moonlighters. Since auction dates are set well in advance, it will be easy to work your auctioneering schedule in with your other activities.

Since it is sometimes difficult to get established as an auctioneer, you might join an established firm if you can find someone who needs an assistant or partner. Another way to get started is to organize a series of *consignment auctions*. Under this arrangement, you will rent a building or outdoor area like the corner of a shopping center parking lot and advertise for people to bring items they want sold at auction. You will then auction off the goods, keeping a percentage of the sales price as your fee. This is an excellent way to gain experience and to get your name known at the same time.

If you like the general idea of earning a part-time income from auctions but prefer not to accept the responsibility of becoming an auctioneer, a related activity may be very suitable.

Auctioneer's helpers assist in displaying goods during the auction and perform other miscellaneous tasks. *Auction clerks* and *cashiers* record each item sold, the amount, and the buyer's name. They also collect amounts due from buyers. No specific training is needed to perform one of these activities, although bonding may be necessary to become a clerk or cashier.

Auction helpers, clerks, and cashiers receive an hourly wage or a percentage of the sale as their pay. Contact a local auctioneer if you are interested in one of these part-time jobs.

Beekeeper

IF YOU have a yearning to get back to the basics and to become closer to nature, you can do it and earn your part-time income as well by becoming a *beekeeper*.

Virtually all part-time beekeepers (officially known as apiarists) look upon raising bees and extracting honey as more than a money-making venture. They view it as an opportunity to study nature, to assist in pollinating the world's food crop, and as a step toward becoming self-sufficient by producing some of their own food.

The principle of raising bees and harvesting honey is quite simple. You buy one or more beehives (also called colonies) and set them up in your backyard, in a field, or near some area where there are flowers and plants. The bees leave the hive to gather pollen and nectar from the flowers' and plants' blossoms and return to make honey. The bees make far more honey than they need for their own food, and you extract the excess for your own use and for sale to others.

No formal education or training is necessary to become a beekeeper, although it is a skill that must be learned. This is accomplished by reading books, working with an experienced beekeeper, and through experience.

Most experts recommend that you enter the beekeeping business gradually by starting out with one to three hives the first year. This will allow you the opportunity to decide if you like this business and will give you a chance to become thoroughly familiar with the activities involved in beekeeping before you engage in a larger operation.

Basic equipment you will need to get started can be purchased from a bee supply company, acquired from a beekeeper who is going out of business, or built through your own efforts. You will need a beehive, which consists of several sections, a bee smoker to calm the bees for when you must work around them, protective clothing, an extractor to remove the honey, and a storage tank to hold it. Then too, you need the bees, which can be purchased from suppliers. Several miscellaneous hand tools will also be needed.

The cost to become fully established with three hives, bees, and all of the equipment you need will probably be several hundred dollars if everything is purchased new from a supplier. If used equipment and supplies are purchased, or if you build your own, the cost will be considerably less. Bee supply companies can be located by checking the yellow pages of a city telephone directory. You may also wish to contact the American Beekeeping Federation, 13637 N.W. 39 Avenue, Gainesville, FL 32606, for information about suppliers and other phases of beekeeping.

The amount of honey harvested from a hive can vary from year to year, with perhaps a minimum of 35 pounds and a maximum of 200. Most likely, production will average around 90 to 110 pounds per hive per year.

Nearly all part-time beekeepers sell their honey directly to consumers in 1- to 10-pound jars. Selling direct in this manner allows you to command perhaps twice the price that would be possible in selling to retailers or wholesalers. The income potential per year can vary considerably depending on the bees' productivity and current prices of honey. In general, you might expect that the income from the first year or two will pay for your bees and equipment and that thereafter most of the earnings will be clear profit. Most likely, it will take 8 to 12 hives to generate a thousand dollars of income from honey sales per year. Commercial beekeepers usually need 500 to 1,000 hives in order to earn a full-time income from honey sales.

You will probably be able to sell all of the honey you produce with ease. Friends, neighbors, relatives, and co-workers are all good prospects that should be contacted personally. You might go door to door (check of a city permit is necessary) or set up a roadside stand. As much as possible, keep a list of customers you can call on from year to year. If your operation and production grows beyond your sales potential through your personal contacts, you can sell to community-minded service organizations for use in a fund-raising project, or sell to health food stores or grocery retailers.

In addition to selling honey, beekeepers can earn money in other ways. One is to rent out the beehives to farmers and other growers to assist in pollination of their crops, which will improve production by perhaps 35 percent. Each hive can handle about one-half acre and is rented for perhaps $20 to $30. When the crops have been pollinated, the hives are moved on to another field or orchard for another rental fee. The income potential from renting bees out for pollination purposes is actually far greater than that which exists from selling the honey.

Selling beeswax is another source of income. Each time the honey is extruded from the honeycomb, the upper layer (or *cap*) of the comb, the beeswax, is cut off to free the honey. The beeswax amounts to only about one percent of the weight received from each extrusion but it sells at a price that is approximately twice the rate received per pound for honey. The beeswax is sold to art supply stores, natural food stores, or bee supply companies.

Raising bees for sale to other beekeepers is another possibility. Ordinarily a package of 10,000 to 12,000 workers and one queen bee are sold, or you might specialize in raising and selling queen bees only.

Bees require attention, but nothing like that which must be ordinarily given in raising other living things. In the spring, you will repair old hives and set up new ones. You will examine the hives, clean them, and move them to a new location, if necessary. On a year-round basis, you will examine the hives for disease and make sure that they do not become overcrowded, or the bees will become upset and leave in a swarm. In the fall and winter, it is necessary to check if the bees have enough honey stored up to last until more is produced in the spring. If not, they should be fed honey or a sugar-water mixture. Throughout the winter, you will need to check on the bees once every week or two.

A country location is ideal for raising bees, but many bee-keepers live in the suburbs and quite a number even live in cities.

Generally, no licenses or permits are required to raise bees, although in some states an inspector may review your operation annually. Often, cities or counties have zoning regulations pertaining to where bees may or may not be kept. Usually no license or permit is required to sell honey, but a label should be attached to the containers showing the name and address of the producer and the weight in pounds and ounces. Check with your State Department of Agriculture, the city clerk, and county recorder to see if any regulations exist that pertain to your intended bee-keeping operation.

Beekeeping can be an ideal family project and is an excellent way to teach children the lessons of nature and business at the same time. For adults, it can be enjoyable and profitable. The business can be easily expanded by adding more hives until bee-keeping occupies the amount of time and provides the amount of income you find desirable.

For more information on beekeeping, you can contact the

Eastern Apicultural Society of North America, 157 Five Point Road, Colts Neck, NJ 07722, or Western Apicultural Society of North America, 2882 East Standish, Anaheim, CA 92806.

Bookkeeping

CALCULATE the answer to this question: If net sales are $1,000, cost of goods sold is $600, and operating expenses are $300, what is net income?

If $100 flashes to your mind as the answer, you apparently have some knowledge of bookkeeping terminology and procedures. If you have enough knowledge in this area, you can become a part-time *bookkeeper.*

Many small businesses, including hair-styling salons, specialty retailers, repair shops, service stations, and home businesses do not have a high enough business volume to warrant hiring a full-time bookkeeper or accountant. This means that the owner or manager must then do the books, or one of the regular employees, if there are any, must do them. Of all the activities involved in operating a small business, bookkeeping is often one of the least favorite, least understood, and most neglected. That is why many small business operators rely upon a part-time bookkeeper.

You can operate your bookkeeping service in one of two ways. One is to go to your client's place of business on a regular schedule and do the work there. The other is to periodically, say once a week, pick up your client's invoices, statements, canceled checks, and other records, and take them to your office or home for recording. On the next visit, you will return the materials and pick up the new data for processing. You might provide your service for one client only, or you might offer a public bookkeeping service, handling several clients.

The level of bookkeeping skill required will vary with the type and variety of activities you perform. If you simply record day-to-day transactions in an existing set of records, no formal training may be required. A "feel" for business, the ability to follow directions, and common sense may be sufficient qualifications. On the other hand, if the bookkeeping system is complicated and if there are many unusual transactions, formal training will probably be a prerequisite. In many cases, a year of high school bookkeeping or two or three college accounting courses may furnish an adequate background.

As the difficulty level of the transactions to be recorded increases, likewise your need for specialized training increases. One rule to follow is that you should never attempt to tackle a bookkeeping job for which you do not have adequate knowledge. Either turn down the job or upgrade your skills so you become competent to do the work. Additional training can be obtained from daytime or evening accounting courses offered at various colleges and business schools in your area.

Unless your skills are well advanced, your activities will probably be limited to recording daily transactions. Your client should then have a bona fide accountant perform the more complicated end-of-the-period activities, prepare the financial statements, and complete the necessary income tax forms.

In addition to operating your own bookkeeping service, good possibilities exist to work for an established accounting or bookkeeping firm part-time. Often, these firms have peak work periods during the year when they are conducting audits or performing fiscal year-end activities. Then too, the situation often occurs where a firm has more work than its regular staff can handle but not enough to hire an additional full-time employee. In order to be a qualified employee for an accounting or bookkeeping firm, you will most likely need to have formal training in bookkeeping or accounting and/or have substantial work experience.

A related, but still different, activity in the bookkeeping area is that of an *income tax preparer*. In order to be successful here, your knowledge must be thorough and up to date. You can study on your own but might be best advised to obtain formal training. A sound background in bookkeeping and accounting funda- mentals and one or two courses in income tax preparation should qualify you to prepare basic tax returns. Additional training will be necessary to be able to tackle more difficult returns.

You can offer an *income tax preparation service* of your own, or you might find it more comforting to work for an established accounting or tax-preparation firm. Since the tax season is by far the busiest time of the year for accountants, many of them will welcome the chance to hire a well-qualified assistant. The income you earn in this three-and-a-half month season may well provide you with the year's additional moonlighting income you require.

If you operate your own bookkeeping service, you can charge at an hourly rate, or quote your clients a contracted price per week or month. Income tax preparation fees are normally based upon the amount of time required to prepare the tax return, with some consideration often given to the difficulty level and number of attached schedules. Set your rates according to those charged by others in your community for similar services. This can vary widely, from perhaps two to five times the minimum wage rate for regular bookkeeping services and a higher rate, perhaps five to ten times the minimum wage rate, for income tax preparation.

If you work for an established accounting firm, performing general bookkeeping services, you will probably be paid on an hourly basis, at perhaps three to five times the minimum wage rate. If you prepare tax returns for an established firm, you will probably be paid a percentage of what your employer charges customers or you will be paid a flat amount per return com- pleted. Therefore, if you work efficiently, you can earn at a high rate.

Whether you operate your own bookkeeping service or work for someone else, excellent possibilities exist for a steady, year-round income, with the additional opportunity for a "bonus" during the income tax season. A strong advantage of moonlighting in the bookkeeping and tax-preparation field is that it is virtually inflation-proof and recession-proof. When times are good and business is booming, businesses *really* need bookkeeping and income tax assistance, and when times are bad and business is sagging, they *really, really* need it.

Business Employee

THE FIRST thought that comes to many people's minds when they hear the term *moonlighting,* is of someone working at a second job, part-time as a *business employee.* There is good reason for this—it is one of the most popular forms of moonlighting.

Almost any type of business is suitable for you to consider for a part-time job, as long as it does not result in a conflict of interest with your regular job and is not out of character for you. Several good possibilities are discussed below.

Bartender: This one is listed first, because if you are a skilled bartender you can get a part-time job in virtually any community in the country at any time you want. It's not that there is necessarily such a high turnover among bartenders but rather that there are so many nightclubs, bars, restaurants, country clubs, private clubs, hotels, and other places where you can employ this skill. That, and the fact that many of these establishments are open for business 15, 16, or more hours per day, thus needing a large staff. Private parties provide another good possibility for employment.

To be a successful bartender, you need several skills. First is the knowledge of the ingredients of a wide range of cocktails, committed to memory, and the ability to mix the drinks quickly and accurately. Second is the stamina to work long hours on your feet. Third is the composure to perform efficiently under pressure. Fourth, but not last in importance, is an understanding of people, a pleasing personality, and conversational ability.

The technical skill of how to mix drinks can be learned through self study and experimentation, but it is best learned by attending a short-term bartending school.

Waiter or Waitress: This one is listed second for the same reason that bartending is listed first—there is a tremendous demand for waiters and waitresses, and an efficient, alert person can almost always find a part-time job anywhere. This line of work doesn't appeal to you, you say. Well, like anything else, it's not for everyone, but there are several excellent advantages. Perhaps foremost of these is that no formal training is ordinarily required, although many managers prefer experience in the area. A lack of experience should be no major handicap, however, since many of the personal relations and organizational skills used in your regular full-time job will carry over.

Another advantage is the income potential. A combination of an hourly wage, which is usually low, plus tips, which can be high, often provides an outstanding hourly income. The amount that is earned in tips is largely dependent upon the type of business establishment and upon your personality, efficiency, appearance, and manner.

Working as a waiter or waitress part-time can provide a nice change of pace from your regular routine. You will meet many interesting people and will have an excellent opportunity to hone your human relations skills.

Retail Store Employee: Many retail stores are open 12 hours or more per day. Thus, if a position is staffed with a full-time employee working 8 hours, there are 4 hours left over. Often, these 4 hours are covered by part-time employees. Almost any type of retail store is a possibility, with those dealing in gifts, clothing, hardware, sporting goods, food, books, baked goods, shoes, sound equipment, and records as likely candidates. Specialty shops dealing in health foods, artworks, jewelry, and the like, and also convenience stores and gasoline service stations hold good potential as well.

Primarily, your duties will include assisting customers, collecting payment for goods sold, and operating the cash register. You might also become involved in stocking shelves, taking inventory, and other miscellaneous tasks.

Although a business background is an asset, it is usually not a necessity. A pleasing personality, pleasant appearance, willingness to work, alertness, and assertiveness are usually qualities that will impress a manager enough to hire you.

Besides offering good opportunity for regular part-time work, retail businesses provide potential for employment during peak periods such as the Christmas rush, during special promotional events, and when seasonal sales are conducted. A side benefit of working at a retail business is that often the employees, including part-timers, are granted a discount on the merchandise purchased at the store for their own use.

Financial Institution Employee: The days of the 9:00 A.M. to 3:00 P.M. banker are long gone in most communities. Also gone are the highly conservative, restrained, low-key, noncompetitive banking attitudes. Today, banks and other financial institutions are in head-to-head, aggressive competition with each other for customers, just like other businesses. This means that financial institutions are open more hours and are offering more services than ever before. The result is that they need more employees than ever before, and many of them are very amenable to the idea of hiring moonlighters.

Commercial banks, savings and loan associations, industrial banks, mutual savings banks, credit unions, small loan companies, and almost any other financial institutions are good possibilities for employment.

Duties you might perform include operating a drive-up teller window, overseeing automated equipment, taking loan applications, processing checks, collecting overdue accounts, or performing secretarial and bookkeeping activities. Some of these positions require a combination of training and experience, while others are entry-level jobs.

Paramount among the qualifications necessary to secure a part-time job at a financial institution are honesty, integrity, and an unblemished background. Attitude, maturity, personality, and appearance also play a big part in the employee-selection process.

Financial institutions are ordinarily looked upon as being among the most stable of all business enterprises. Therefore, if you land a part-time job with one of them, good opportunity exists for long-term employment and for development of the position into a full-time career.

Hotel or Motel Employee: Since hotels and motels offer services around the clock, many opportunities exist for the moonlighter. These include jobs in security, cleaning, laundry, grounds maintenance, public relations, and general maintenance. Other positions are cook, restaurant hostess, waiter or waitress, bartender, reservations desk operator, night auditor, switchboard operator, porter, vehicle parking attendant, and recreation director. Still others include gift shop operator, rest room attendant, shoeshine stand operator, and limousine chauffeur. And there are other possibilities too!

Since hotels and motels are in the hospitality industry, one of the main qualifications is that you should be hospitable. A pleasing personality, willingness to be helpful, and cordial attitude are necessities. Also, honesty and integrity are musts, since you may be entrusted with a guest's property or may be in the guests' rooms alone.

Other Possibilities: The preceding opportunities for business employees are listed separately since each is a large area with much potential. However, many other possibilities exist that may match your interests, abilities, and time schedule. Some of these include car-wash attendant, florist shop flower arranger, greenhouse or nursery employee, glazier (window and glass installer), or movie theater employee. Excellent part-time employment opportunities also exist at airport terminals, sports arenas, and resorts.

Entry-level income for a business employee is often at or near the minimum wage rate, although many positions pay two or three times that amount. Many times, fringe benefits, employee discounts, commission incentives, and tips will increase the earnings to a very acceptable level.

Carpet Layer

Look down. Most likely, your feet are resting on carpet, linoleum, or inlaid flooring. If you consider that nearly every house, office building, school, church, retail store, apartment building, and other structure in the country has some type of similar flooring, it is easy to imagine the great potential that can exist to moonlight as a *carpet layer*.

You have probably seen a carpet layer or two in action, so you already know what they do. They install carpet, and perhaps other types of flooring as well. Is this a complicated task? No, not really, but it must be learned before you can go into business.

Carpet laying is not learned by reading a book or by watching someone else do it, although these are helpful; it is learned by doing. One way to learn is through on-the-job training by working with an experienced carpet layer. After just a few installations, you will get the basic idea and in the matter of a few days you will be able to make installations yourself. With a few weeks' additional experience, you will be able to tackle almost any job alone.

Attending a training school offered by a floor-covering mill or distributor is another way to learn the craft. These sessions may last anywhere from a day to a week. They are usually free of charge, since mills and distributors are eager to help prepare qualified people to install their products, which in turn should increase sales. A local carpet dealer should be able to get you in touch with someone who will soon be offering a training school, or you can make direct contact with carpet mills and distributors. It might be helpful to know that most U.S. carpet mills are located in the state of Georgia.

Basically, your carpet-laying activities will include rolling out the carpet (and perhaps carpet pad), positioning it, stretching it tightly, and gluing and/or tacking it into place. If you install linoleum and inlaid flooring, one of your most precise activities must be to measure and cut accurately, since it cannot be stretched that extra inch or so to make it fit.

Equipment you will need includes a carpet stretcher, tack hammer, cutting knife, and a few miscellaneous hand tools for spreading glue and other odd jobs. The investment is relatively small, with only a few hundred dollars needed to become adequately equipped. You should also obtain liability insurance that will cover any damage you do to a customer's property, like scratching furniture that you move. The cost is low and the insurance can be obtained from your regular agent.

You are now ready for your first job. You can work for an established carpet layer or work for one specific carpet dealer. An advantage of working for someone else is that they will line up the work and you will not need to concern yourself with advertising, promoting, and other business details. Most likely, they will pay you at a set rate per square yard of flooring installed, which should result in earnings of two to four times the minimum wage rate.

Another possibility is to operate as a free-lance carpet layer. Here you can offer your services to many different carpet dealers, lumberyards, decoration centers, contractors, and individuals. Personal contact with retailers who sell floor coverings should land many jobs. Advertisements in your local newspaper should bring many orders from individuals who have purchased their own floor coverings from a discount dealer, through the mail, or from a dealer who does not offer an installation service.

You can require that your customers have the carpet delivered by the dealer they purchased it from or that your customers pick it up themselves. You might want to, however, secure a vehicle suitable for hauling carpet since it will make your service more attractive. A van, station wagon, or pickup truck with a topper should be satisfactory.

Ordinarily, carpet layers charge a set amount per square yard installed. Since linoleum and inlaid flooring are usually more difficult and time consuming to install than carpet, a higher rate is charged for them. Usually, a minimum fee is charged for a small but time-consuming job like a bathroom floor. Stairways are usually charged for at a set amount per step.

The rate per square yard varies from community to community, but several dollars per yard for carpet, twice that for linoleum, and three times that for inlaid flooring is a general indication. An experienced carpet layer may be able to lay as much as 40 square yards of carpet an hour in a wide-open, uncluttered area. Perhaps 10 to 15 square yards of carpet can be installed per hour in an average home. The production rate for installing other types of flooring is considerably lower, but this is compensated for by the higher rate charged. It is therefore easy to see that a carpet layer's earnings potential can be high.

Being a carpet layer can be hard work, but an advantage that you have as a moonlighter is that you don't need to take every job that comes along. You can pick and choose to some extent and take only those that will be easy, fast, and profitable.

A natural extention of the carpet-laying profession is to sell carpet. No, you don't need a huge warehouse or even a retail display area. You can sell exclusively from *carpet samples*. You will buy or rent the samples from mills or distributors, show them to your potential customers, make the sale, and submit the order. The mill or distributor will ship the floor covering to you, and you will install it.

If you buy directly from the mills, your prices will be lower, but delivery time is longer, perhaps 7 to 14 days. If you buy from distributors, overnight delivery is possible in many cases.

Selling floor coverings is an excellent way to increase your income and to provide an extra service for your customers as well.

Chimney Sweep

Here's a little riddle: What's black on the outside and green on the inside? Give up? It's a *chimney sweep*! You don't get it, you say. Well, the black is from the black suit worn by the chimney sweep (not from the soot as you might suspect) and the green is from all of the cash stuffed inside the chimney sweep's suit pockets. Translation: Being a chimney sweep can be a very profitable way to moonlight.

Perhaps, you say, chimney sweeps are a thing of the past. Yes, a century ago, when homes were heated with woodburning stoves and fireplaces, chimney sweeps were very popular, particularly in Europe. That factor is exactly what makes the chimney sweep popular today. As the cost of natural gas and other heating fuels has skyrocketed, homeowners have chosen to return more and more to the basics for heating their homes—to woodburners. Fireplaces and woodburning stoves and furnaces are more popular than ever and their use continues to grow.

There is a problem, though, with using these woodburners. That is, the extreme heat caused by burning wood (or coal) causes soot and creosote to build up in the chimney flue. If this soot and creosote is not cleaned out periodically, the result can be disastrous—a smoke-filled home or a chimney fire that may spread to the rest of the house.

To eliminate these possibilities, the chimney should be checked every year and it should be cleaned regularly. If the woodburner is used frequently, an annual cleaning is probably necessary; if it is used sparingly, a cleaning every two or three years may be sufficient. What all this amounts to is that there is a tremendous need for people who check and clean chimneys.

Sweeping chimneys is not a difficult task, nor is it as messy as you might imagine. Most homeowners, however, lack the knowledge of how to do it, don't have the desire to do it, or don't possess adequate equipment to do it. Therefore, they hire a professional chimney sweep.

As a chimney sweep, your tasks are quite well defined—clean all of the soot and creosote out of the chimney. There is no one right way to do this and you can probably develop your own techniques. Basically though, the chimney is either cleaned from the top, by going up on the roof, or it is cleaned from the bottom. In either case, a stiff brush attached to a long handle, or some similar object, is swabbed up and down in the flue until all of the soot and creosote is knocked loose. Then the residue is vacuumed up or shoveled into paper bags and removed from the premises.

Precaution must be taken so that you do not allow soot particles to drift into the home and so you do not track dirt with your feet or equipment. This can be eliminated by carefully spreading a drop cloth around your work area inside the home and by continually running an industrial vacuum cleaner near the inside work area.

For a small investment, you can design and build much of your own equipment, or you can buy specially designed chimney-sweeping gear from a manufacturer, also at a modest cost. You will also need a ladder, industrial vacuum cleaner, drop cloths, and a few miscellaneous hand tools.

Time required to clean a chimney varies with the type of equipment used, technique used, and your experience and skill. A range of one to two hours per chimney is probably average.

Now the important part—how much can a person earn as a chimney sweep? This may surprise you, but an average of $40 to $50 per chimney is not unusual, and more is charged in some localities. If there is more than one chimney in the home, the regular rate is charged for the first one and a reduced rate of one-fourth to one-half the regular rate is charged for each additional one. This means that earnings of several hundred dollars can be earned per week on a part-time basis.

As with any business venture, promotion of your chimney-sweeping service is necessary. Regular advertising methods can be used, but the simplest, least expensive, most effective, and most fun way to promote your activity is so obvious that some people might overlook it. That is, dress like a *real* chimney sweep. Wear a black suit (with tails even) and a black top hat. The very sight of you will be your best advertisement, and word of mouth will bring many new customers who are intrigued by the novelty of it all.

For more information on how to become a chimney sweep and how to obtain professional equipment, contact the National Chimney Sweep Guild, P.O. Box 1078, Merrimack, NH 03054.

Cleaning Service

How would you like to whiz through cleaning tasks like vacuuming, dusting, and scrubbing floors—and all the while have a smile on your face? Impossible, you say. Not at all. It *is* possible—when you are cleaning someone else's home or business and are getting paid for it—by providing a professional *cleaning service*.

One type of operation for you to consider is a *housecleaning service*. Here you can perform light housecleaning like vacuuming, dusting, waxing furniture, and the like. You might also offer additional services such as window washing and floor waxing. You can provide this service to one or more clients on a regular basis, you can operate a free-lance housecleaning service, or you can do both.

If you serve regular customers, you will clean for them periodically, usually once or twice per week. Potential customers include the elderly, handicapped, well-to-do, and busy families where both husband and wife work.

If you offer a free-lance housecleaning service, you will perform your activities for customers whenever they need your help, rather than on a regular basis. Potential customers include homeowners preparing for a special event like a graduation, wedding, party, or something else for which the home needs to be in extra-special condition. Landlords and real estate agents are also good contacts, since a home vacated by a tenant or owner may need some sprucing up before it is shown to another prospect. Lending institutions, who on occasion repossess homes, are also good potential customers.

A *custodial service* is another avenue through which your cleaning services can be provided. Here your clients will be businesses and other organizations rather than individuals. Any small operation that does not merit a full-time custodial staff is a potential client. These include retail stores, real estate agencies, business offices, churches, private clubs, and lodges. In fact, there are probably hundreds of potential customers in your immediate area.

Your activities will include cleaning, vacuuming, dusting, and waxing. In addition, you might empty wastebaskets, wash window interiors, water plants, and mow the lawn. In some cases, if you are a church custodian, for instance, you might rearrange furnishings, set up tables, and so forth for the next day's activities.

The volume of traffic through the building will largely determine the amount of custodial services a customer will require. Retail businesses, with a steady flow of daily customers, may need daily vacuuming and mopping, while dusting and some of the other cleaning activities can be done periodically. Relatively inactive offices, or those where most traffic is confined to a reception and service counter area, may require attention only once or twice per week.

In some cases, no investment in equipment or supplies may be required to establish your housecleaning service or custodial service—your client will furnish everything you need. In other cases, you may need to provide a broom, mop, bucket, dustpan, heavy-duty vacuum cleaner, and an assortment of cleaning cloths, cleaning agents, and other miscellaneous articles. Your start-up cost will be very low.

Personal qualities like the ability to work without supervision and the desire to do a first-rate, conscientious job are necessary. Honesty is a must since you may be entrusted to work alone in a home while the owner is away or in a business establishment before or after normal business hours.

The charge for your cleaning services can be set at an hourly rate or at a flat amount per week or per month. In either case, your earnings might range from minimum wage to perhaps two or three times that amount. Several hundred dollars can easily be earned per month on a part-time basis.

It is entirely possible that you may need only one or two good clients to keep you as busy as you want to be. Undoubtedly, there will be many more clients available to you than that, and you may therefore want to expand your horizons to becoming a *cleaning service contractor*. Here, you would contract the housecleaning and commercial cleaning jobs and hire other moonlighters to do them.

In this position, your role will be supervisory and you will need to engage dependable and conscientious workers, and you will need to occasionally review their work. You will keep a percentage of the income received from your customers, thus developing a strong income potential.

Another moonlighting way to "clean up" is to become a *used-*

car lot attendant. This is the official name for someone who cleans up used cars that are acquired by a new- or used-car dealer.

A *window-washing service* is also worth considering. Here you would wash windows for regular customers on a periodic basis or offer a free-lance service for individuals and businesses.

Another opportunity in a related area to providing a cleaning service is to operate a *carpet-cleaning and floor-wax service.* With this business, you would use heavy-duty professional equipment to shampoo carpets and wax, polish, and buff hard-surface floors. Most likely, you would also clean and vacuum drapes, stuffed furniture, and similar items found in the home and businesses.

Many homeowners will use your service regularly once or twice per year, and many people will call upon you prior to important at-home receptions or parties. Businesses of all kinds can use your service on a regular basis, anywhere from once a week to once a year. Your best business clients will undoubtedly be those smaller operations that find it impractical to purchase their own equipment or who need this service only infrequently.

In addition to your carpet-cleaning and floor-wax service, you can also offer a *disaster restoration service.* Here, you would vacuum dry a flooded basement, clean up the smoke and water damage after a fire, and clean up and restore property after some other type of disaster.

You can either operate as an independent or as a franchise holder. As an independent, you would purchase your own equipment and supplies from one or more commercial suppliers and establish your own business under your own name. As a franchise holder, you would purchase a franchise and the equipment and supplies from a nationally or regionally known company. If the idea of obtaining a franchise sounds appealing, you might contact Servicemaster, 2300 Warrenville Road, Downers Grove, IL 60515.

Regardless of how your business is organized, your equipment requirements will be basically the same. You will need a heavy-duty carpet shampooer, one or more vacuum cleaners, and a unit to scrub, wax, and polish hard-surface floors. Commercial cleaning agents and a variety of brushes and miscellaneous cleaning materials will also be needed. This may require an investment of several thousand dollars, but some of the companies who sell franchises have installment plans whereby payments can be made monthly.

A limited amount of specialized knowledge and training is required to offer this service. If you buy a franchise, the company will probably offer a school of say two weeks' duration, which will include business and management training as well as hands-on technical training. If you set up your own independent operation, the companies who sell you the equipment will probably offer a short but effective training course in its operation.

You can set your rates per square foot of carpet or floor that is cleaned. The rates should include the cost of all materials and provide you with a generous hourly wage, say three to five times the minimum wage rate. Working just a few hours per day, two to three days per week, will yield earnings of several hundred dollars per month.

Coin Dealer

How's YOUR *numismatic* knowledge? If it is high, you need look no further to find a way to moonlight. The perfect opportunity awaits you as a numismatist, or *coin dealer*.

As a coin dealer, you will buy, sell, and trade coins. There is far more to this profession, however, than these regular retail activities. One of the most important is a knowledge of coins and of their value. A coin dealer must be able to buy wisely and sell at a profit. This may sound simple enough, but in reality it takes much experience to become an expert coin buyer. The reason for this is the fact that there are no established prices for coins and that any coin is worth only what someone will pay for it.

Prices shown in coin books and collector's magazines are only guidelines. Actual sales prices may be far higher or lower.

Because there is such a wide range of collectibles, including American, foreign, ancient, and rare coins, most dealers specialize in one or two areas. Some dealers also handle paper money, tokens, or other items of value.

An important, and often exciting, part of a coin dealer's activities is that of seeking out coins to acquire. This is done by attending coin shows, conventions, flea markets, and coin auctions. Often, it involves tracking down individuals who have coin collections and buying one item or the entire collection. Personal contacts with customers will result in many good finds. Then too, you can advertise in city newspapers or coin collector's magazines and newsletters to locate coins to buy.

The selling aspect of a coin dealer's business is a retail function that often requires an active approach. Rather than simply waiting and hoping that buyers will come to you, it is often necessary to seek out customers. One good technique is to attend coin shows, conventions, flea markets, and other similar events where coin buyers gather. You should also keep accurate lists of collectors and the type of coins in which they specialize. Then, when you acquire a new coin, you can check your files and contact the right prospect in the hope of making a quick sale. You can also advertise in specialized coin collector's publications.

Coin collecting is not a topic that a person can learn overnight or through a short cram course. Usually, an interest in coin collecting, and the progression to becoming a coin dealer, evolves naturally and slowly over a period of several years. A person becomes interested in coins, and this interest leads them to exploring and learning more. Eventually, when they have learned enough to become knowledgeable in some area and have accumulated a large enough collection, they start trading, buying, and selling. Before they know it, they are bona fide dealers.

Anyone wishing to speed up this normally slow and gradual process of becoming a coin collector and dealer can do so through active study. There are hundreds of books on the topic that are worth reading. Also, regular visits to coin-rich museums, coin shows, auctions, and events where coin dealers gather and coins are displayed will be very helpful. Consider joining a coin collector's organization like the American Numismatic Society, Broadway & 156th Street, New York, NY 10032, or the American Numismatic Association, Box 2366, Colorado Springs, CO 80901. They provide information, conduct seminars, hold conventions, and offer other worthwhile services.

An advantage of moonlighting as a coin dealer is that you do not need to acquire a huge inventory like most full-time dealers. You can work into the business slowly, buying and selling a few coins at a time, ploughing back the profits and building up inventory. As the number of coins you handle increases, your profit potential will also grow.

Another advantage of being a part-time coin dealer is that you do not need to have a retail business location. You can if you want to, of course, but you can easily operate out of your home, through mail order, and by attending various coin shows. Very little space is required by a coin collection and your inventory can be easily packed, transported, and displayed.

The type of coins you handle will be largely determined by your personal interests, your financial capabilities, and your contacts. Subsequently, the type of customers you deal with will be largely determined by the type of coins you handle. Your earnings potential will be determined by both these factors.

For instance, if you deal with relatively ordinary and easily obtainable coins, most of your customers will be beginning hobbyists and your sales amount and profit per item will be relatively low. If you deal in more difficult-to-obtain coins, your profit potential per sale may be greater. Any mode of operation can be satisfactory as long as it matches your interests, personality, goals, and financial abilities.

Good potential exists for a knowledgeable part-time coin dealer to earn good money right away. Most likely, your income will increase steadily from year to year as you gain experience and develop more contacts. The possibility (and hope!) always exists, of course, to "find" a rare coin at a bargain price. Since some coins sell for well over a million dollars each, a single transaction could produce profits equal to or greater than a normal lifetime's earnings.

For the person who enjoys coin collecting, becoming a coin dealer is the ideal part-time job. In fact, actively pursuing your hobby will be such a pleasure that it will not seem like a job at all.

The life of a *philatelist* is very similar to that of a numistatist. Translated, this means that if you are a stamp collector, or want to be, you should consider moonlighting as a *stamp dealer*. Here you would buy, sell, and trade stamps, using many of the same techniques and procedures used by a coin dealer. If you are interested in this exciting area, contact the American Stamp Dealer's Association, Inc., 5 Dakota Drive, Suite 102, Lake Success, NY 11042, for more information.

Collection Agent

Do YOUR personal attributes include being persuasive yet unyielding, empathetic yet firm, aggressive yet restrained, and demanding yet fair? Do you have honesty, integrity, diplomacy, and tact? Well, if you possess this almost seemingly impossible list of credentials, you may be ideally suited to moonlight as a *collection agent*.

As a collection agent, you will collect overdue accounts from debtors. You can operate independently, or you can work as an employee for an established collection agency. In either case, your collection activities are basically the same.

There are two primary functions performed by a collection

agent. The first is to locate businesses or others who have over-due accounts receivable (amounts owed to them) that they have been unable to collect. You must then convince them that you will be able to collect a substantial portion of these amounts for them. The second function is to contact the debtors and collect the money.

Your potential clients are many. These include virtually all retail businesses, professionals, and even colleges and govern-ment agencies. A big field alone exists in collecting overdue government student loans. Doctors, dentists, and others in the health professions are particularly good potential clients since they often have huge accounts receivable and are lackadaisical in their own collection procedures.

Basically, your service works like this: The client turns over to you all of his overdue accounts receivable. You then contact the debtors, putting forth your best efforts to collect the amounts due. For providing your service, you receive a percentage of the amount collected and your client gets the rest.

The percentage you receive depends upon the quality of your client's accounts receivable. Experience shows that the longer an account has been overdue, the more difficult it is to collect; the shorter time an account is overdue, the easier it is to collect. Therefore, your collection-fee percentage on long-overdue ac-counts will be higher than on those overdue a shorter time. As a general guide, you might charge a fee of 25 to 33 1/3 percent of amounts collected on accounts 30 to 180 days overdue and charge 50 percent or even higher on accounts six months or more overdue. In all cases, your income is calculated as a per-centage of amounts collected; if you collect nothing, you receive nothing.

Another possibility is to buy your client's accounts receivable outright, paying perhaps 50 percent or less of their recorded value. The client's advantage is that cash is received right away. Your advantage is that, if you collect a high percentage of that due, you can earn a substantial amount. Your risk is that there is no guarantee of what amount will be collectible and you could conceivably collect less than you paid for the accounts. Most collection agents work on a percentage of the amounts collected rather than buying accounts outright.

Regardless of whether you work on a percentage or buy the accounts outright, your client will be concerned about the methods, techniques, and tactics you will use to collect the accounts. Obviously, if you are rude, dishonest, unscrupulous, or undiplomatic, you will ruin your client's chances of ever doing business with those customers again. Therefore, you must convince your clients that you will use ethical, legal, fair, and professional methods in your collections.

Procedures used by collection agents are controlled by the Fair Debt Collection Procedures Act. This federal legislation describes exactly what may or may not be done, and every collection agent must become thoroughly familiar with its stipulations.

Specifics of the act are too numerous to list here, but methods of making initial contact with the debtor, times when the debtor may not be contacted at home or at work, and types of inquiries that may or may not be made of the debtor's relatives and employer are among those points spelled out. In reality, the act only requires what a legitimate, professional collection agent would or would not do anyway as guided by ethics, fairness, and common sense. A copy of the Fair Credit Collection Procedures Act can be obtained from the Federal Trade Commission, Pennsylvania Avenue at 6th Street N.W., Washington, DC 20580.

Most states also have regulations pertaining to collection agents' practices, licensing, and bonding. The regulations vary from state to state, and you should contact your State Commerce Commission for specifics. Ordinarily, the licensing and bonding requirements are easy to comply with. The other regulations are similar to those of the Federal Fair Credit Collection Procedures Act.

Primarily, your collection activities involve salesmanship. You must convince the debtors that paying their debts is in their own best interests, since doing so will enable them to receive credit more readily in the future. Also, you should appeal to their sense of fairness; that they used the goods or services and now it is only right that they pay for them. In many cases, you may need to set up a payment schedule whereby they pay the debt through a series of weekly or monthly payments.

Very little investment is required to become a collection agent. You will need a typewriter for preparing collection letters to be mailed out and will need a telephone available for business use. You will also need a vehicle for making personal contacts with clients and debtors.

Moonlighting as a collection agent can be very profitable for the amount of time invested. Often, the shock of receiving a letter from a collection agent is enough to jar a debtor into making payment. Then too, strange as it may sound, you may make many good friends from the contacts you make while pursuing the collection of a debt.

If the credit area sounds interesting, you might also consider moonlighting as a *credit investigator*. Here, you would research a credit applicant's background, usually for a credit-reporting agency.

Concessionaire

How would you like to operate your own little business where a carnival-like atmosphere generally prevails, people are mostly in a festive mood, and customers often stand in line to buy your wares? If this sounds like the ideal business climate, you will probably enjoy moonlighting as a *concessionaire*.

As a concessionaire you will operate a concession stand on a year-round, seasonal, or special-event basis selling food, beverages, novelty items, or other goods. Your concession stand might be a small, converted mobile home or trailer that is easily movable, a tentlike structure that is easy to set up and take down, a permanent stand, or a rented facility.

You might operate a lunch wagon that attends every auction, flea market, or Little League ball game and practice session in the area. Perhaps you will travel a route from swimming pool to tennis court to city park selling ice cream products and slush drinks. Maybe you will be a street vendor selling popcorn, hot dogs, or beverages. Perhaps you will service one or more area campgrounds on a daily basis. Maybe you will operate a stand in a shopping center.

Good opportunity exists to make a season's or year's part-time income in a few days by operating a concession stand at a carnival, county fair, state fair, home show, special community celebration, renaissance fair, or similar event. If this appeals to you, you might plan to arrange part of the vacation time from your regular job so that it coincides with a big-drawing event in your area.

You can sell nearly any type of product, including caramel apples, foot-long hot dogs, cotton candy, hats, dolls, helium-filled balloons, trinkets, miniature-size doughnuts, jewelry, and caramel corn. You might sell food slicers, magical cleansers, cutlery, engraved redwood signs, handmade leather goods, homemade crafts, or a thousand other things. Whether it is usual or unusual, ordinary or extraordinary, it is suitable for sale by a concessionaire.

Another possibility to consider is operating a *game stand* like those ordinarily found at carnivals and county fairs. Games like baseball throw, dart throw, ring toss, and bingo are always popular.

If you intend to sell a product, one of the important aspects of establishing your concession stand is to locate suitable suppliers. In particular, investigate each supplier's ability to furnish you with goods on short notice and whether or not it will be permissible for you to return unsold items.

Another important step is to determine what licenses, permits, and authorizations are needed. For example, if you sell a food product, a license will be necessary from the State Department of Agriculture, and a local permit may also be necessary. If you intend to operate your stand within the city limits, a city vendor's permit may be necessary, and you may need explicit authorization to operate at your particular site. If you operate outside the city limits, say at a roadside stand or at farm auctions, a county permit may be required. If you intend to operate a game stand, you must check state, county, and city regulations to see if such activities are legal and if a gambling permit is needed.

If you intend to set up shop at a county fair, home show, or other special event, you will also need authorization from the board or organization sponsoring the affair. Ordinarily, they limit the number of concession stands of each type to a certain number. This is to allow each concessionaire the opportunity to make a fair profit without being overrun by numerous competitors. This is also in the sponsor's best interests, since it keeps concessionaires coming back year after year, paying lease fees or entry fees for the privilege of setting up shop.

Even though your concession stand may be small and is perhaps in operation for only a short time period each year, it should still be organized and operated according to sound business principles. Develop promotional techniques to draw customers to you and provide quality service and products so they will come back again. Even if you only operate seasonally or at special events, people will remember you and will consistently patronize or avoid your stand year after year.

The amount of investment required to establish a concession stand can range from very small to substantial amounts, depending upon the product sold and the length of time for which the stand will be operated. Many can be started for less than $500.

The income from a concession stand can also cover a wide

range. Certainly, the potential exists to make an unbelievably large amount of money in a very short time. Often, well over a thousand dollars can be cleared in a week's time or less at a high-traffic special event. One thing is for certain, operating a concession stand is not dull, and the fast-paced action may be a nice change from your regular routine.

Other moonlighting activities that can be operated from a booth at a carnival or fair, from your home by appointment, or from a small business office are *fortune-teller, astrologer,* and *horoscope reader.* To some people, these terms may conjure up thoughts of voodoo, the occult, and black magic. The informed, however, realize that to become proficient and reliable in one of these areas usually takes intense training and/or special talent. If you develop trustworthy abilities in one of these areas, you will draw many one-time customers who will come to you out of curiosity. You will also develop many regular customers who will patronize you on a weekly or monthly basis, which will provide you with a steady and substantial income.

Consultant

Do you know a lot about a little bit? If so, you can share your expert knowledge with others for a fee, as a *consultant.*

The primary requirement to become a consultant is that you have specialized knowledge in some area, almost any area, that others want to or need to know about. You will study clients' situations and help them reach a beneficial solution. This might involve making recommendations, or, in some cases, simply guiding and channeling the clients' activities and thoughts by questioning and probing until they reach a logical conclusion.

But you don't have any specialized knowledge, you say—nothing that anyone will pay for anyway. Well, maybe—but greater opportunity exists than most people realize. It's often just a matter of identifying your expertise, organizing it into a useful and appealing "package" that can be offered to clients, and promoting your service. Let's look at some of the possibilities.

If you have experience or training in the business field, you can become a *business consultant*. This is a huge market that encompasses retail stores, home businesses, service operations, corporations, and other businesses of all sizes and types. You might specialize in one type of business, such as restaurants or clothing stores, or in one phase of business operation, such as advertising, promotions, or store layout. Your goal as a business consultant is ordinarily to decrease costs, improve efficiency, increase sales, or redirect emphasis, all with one underlying purpose in mind—to increase net income.

If you have knowledge about computers, data processing, or word processing, you can become a *data processing consultant*. Here, you would study the needs of a business, school, or individual and recommend the most appropriate installation and procedures.

The government, at all levels, is one of the biggest users of consultants. If your expertise lies in economics, foreign policy, taxes, law, or many other areas, you might become a *government consultant*. Those who know about solar, wind-powered, or other types of heating systems and methods will find many customers among businesses and individuals. Also, if you know about insulation methods, weather stripping, and other ways to seal a home or business, you can become an *energy conservation consultant* and advise on ways to conserve energy and decrease heating costs.

Good opportunity exists for an *acoustical consultant* who advises contractors and building owners on the best design and materials to use to reduce noise levels and to create the type of sound desired. The types of structures to which this talent can be applied include office buildings, gymnasiums, convention centers, professional recording studios, concert halls, school music rooms, auditoriums, factories, racquetball courts, and many others.

Someone knowledgeable in the financial area can establish a *financial planning service* to advise businesses, organizations, and individuals on budget development, methods of financing major, long-term purchases, and suitable investment opportunities to select.

Many parents of college-bound students will utilize the services of a *scholarship consultant* who knows what scholarships and financial aid are available and knows how to apply for and obtain them.

If you know the ins and outs of applying for grants offered by the federal government and private foundations, you can be a *grant-writing consultant.* Here, you will advise city, county, and state governments, and schools, colleges, and others on how to find out about the grants, complete the application procedures, and secure the funds.

Opportunities to be a consultant are not limited to the rather technical and specialized areas previously mentioned. If you have knowledge in antique or customized automobiles, landscaping, art, coin collecting, retirement programs, income taxes, inheritance taxes, investments, party planning, wedding planning, animal breeding, job application procedures, home businesses, auto repair, or hundreds of other topics, you can develop and operate some type of a part-time consulting business.

Regardless of the area in which you are a consultant, the basic procedures are the same. Much time is spent in gathering information and analyzing your client's circumstances, needs, and goals. You will then make a recommendation or help your clients seek their own solution. Ordinarily, this recommendation is in the form of a written report that identifies the problem and states various alternate answers. You may or may not help institute the recommended plan of action.

Equipment, materials, and supplies needed to be a consultant will vary a great deal from one area to another. In some cases, where you review a client's records or procedures, perhaps only a calculator and a few reference books are needed. In other cases, specialized equipment to test noise levels, mechanical performance, and so on may be necessary.

Clients for your consulting services can be landed through a number of promotional techniques. One of the best is to attend conventions and meetings where people who are interested in your area gather. If you can get on the program as a speaker or panel-discussion participant, so much the better.

You should also make contacts with business suppliers, financial institutions, lending agencies, professional organizations, Chamber of Commerce offices, accountants, and others who are connected in some way to your area of expertise. Often, they will have clients or associates who will be in need of advice and assistance, and it will be beneficial to everyone involved for them to recommend your services.

If the promotional aspect of consulting does not appeal to you, contact an established consulting firm to see if they can use your services. The benefit to you here is that they will line up the clients, and your activities will be limited to the actual consulting.

Consultant's fees are ordinarily set at a per-hour or per-day rate. It is not unusual for top senior consultants to charge well over $1,000 per day, and even junior consultants may earn several hundred dollars per day. A beginning consultant working with small clients may, of course, initially earn considerably lower rates. The nature of your consulting and the value your client will receive from it might serve as a guide in setting your rates. For instance, if you are giving technical advice on design of a building for acoustics control, you will be able to charge more than if you specialize in advising people how to plant potatoes in a home garden.

Some consultants operate on a flat fee plus a percentage of the savings or increased profits that result from their recommendations. Regardless of the method of setting your rates, it should be discussed with your client in advance, and your entire agreement should be in writing.

Consulting is the favorite moonlighting activity of many people (university professors, particularly), since much of the work is done on a very flexible time schedule in the consultant's home or office. Also, because of the specialized nature of the work, the earnings potential can be phenomenal. It is not unusual for a person who moonlights as a consultant to earn as much or more from consulting activities, in far less time, than from a regular, full-time job. Often, however, it is the nature and prestige of the full-time job that makes it possible to be a well-paid consultant.

Driver

IF YOU feel at ease behind the wheel of a vehicle, have steady nerves, and good human relations skills, several good moonlighting opportunities await you as a professional *driver*.

One possibility is as a *school bus driver,* where you would drive a morning, noon, or afternoon route. Often, an appealing feature of this part-time job is that you will have all holidays off, will get a lengthy Christmas break, and may get a summer vacation as well. You might also drive a school bus to haul athletes, musicians, and fans to contests, tournaments, and the like, and to transport classes on field trips.

Being a *city bus driver* is another possibility. You might work one or two days or nights per week as a substitute for regular drivers on their days off or to help over vacation time. Being a *standby driver* is another possibility, where you will fill in when extra buses are needed on regular routes because of unusually heavy traffic. You might also be assigned your own regular route that is operated less than full time, say perhaps four hours per day.

Companies providing chartered bus services are a good source of part-time employment as a *chartered bus driver*. Businesses, social organizations, churches, schools, colleges, travel agencies, and others contract for the exclusive use of a bus for an afternoon, a week, a month, or other time period.

The destination may be relatively close, can consist of a cross-country tour, or could be anything in between. It will often be possible to drive one or two days per week—on days off from your regular job. If you want, you can probably spend all or part of your regular-job vacation time driving a chartered bus on a long-distance trip, seeing the country, and getting paid for it.

On occasion, private businesses also have need for a part-time *shuttle bus driver* to haul workers to and from a remote work site such as a logging camp or mining site.

Other opportunities exist to use your driving skills besides driving a bus. These include being a *moving van driver* or *truck driver* on short- or long-distance hauls for a business in your area.

If you like driving but would like to stay away from the larger vehicles like buses and trucks, many possibilities still exist for you. In virtually every community with a population of 15,000 or more, opportunities exist to become a part-time *taxicab driver*. Also, many hotels located in cities with an active airport offer a limousine service, for which you could become a *chauffeur* to transport guests between the hotel and airport. You might also perform as a chauffeur for a company, wealthy family, or limousine service, spelling their regular drivers on their days off. Other possibilities exist to become an *ambulance driver* or *funeral limousine driver*.

If you live in an extremely popular part of the country, like some areas of Colorado, Arizona, or California, a unique opportunity to earn money as a driver may exist. The opportunity is spawned by the fact that more people move into these areas than move out, and many of those moving in do so via rented trucks. Therefore, rental agencies in those areas often end up with huge inventories and they get larger all the time. Consequently, drivers are hired to drive the extra trucks to outlying areas where the reverse of this situation exists.

A chauffeur's license is ordinarily required if you drive a vehicle for hire or if the vehicle is over a certain size, say five tons. In order to obtain a chauffeur's license, the applicant must ordinarily pass a practical driving exam, and must have good eyesight, good hearing, and cannot be color-blind. Each state has its own age requirements, often with a minimum age of 18, for drivers who deal in intrastate commerce (driving within the state only). Those who drive in interstate commerce (crossing state lines) must be 21 years old. A specialized license, such as a taxicab license from the city or state taxicab authority, may be necessary for specific types of driving. Check with your State Department of Transportation to determine what licensing is necessary.

Special training in safety, first aid, and other areas may be necessary if you plan to transport people. Likewise, if you drive in interstate commerce, extra training in U.S. Department of Transportation rules, regulations, and procedures may be necessary.

Since duties such as collecting fares, punching tickets, handling baggage, and completing reports are often part of the occupation, many companies provide a short-term training session for all new drivers. Human relations training is often a part of these sessions.

An advantage of moonlighting as a driver is that you ordinarily have very little investment, since the vehicle is supplied by your employer. The cost of obtaining a chauffeur's license is relatively low, as are the annual or biennial renewal fees.

Drivers are paid according to a variety of arrangements. A school bus driver might be paid a monthly salary; a city bus driver may be paid an hourly wage; a charter bus driver can expect to receive a flat amount for the trip or a certain amount per mile; and a taxicab driver might receive a share of all fares collected, plus tips. The earnings will vary with the type of driving, but, in general, it will probably be in the range of two to four times the minimum wage rate.

Several nondriving part-time job possibilities exist in the transportation field. One of these is as a *taxicab dispatcher*, where you take customer's telephone requests for a taxicab and relate them to the driver nearest to the rider's origin. Another is as a *freight clerk,* who helps load a truck with goods such as milk, soft drinks, or bread, often in the off hours, so it will be ready to go when the driver reports to work. Persons employed in these positions are ordinarily paid an hourly wage.

Driver-Training Instructor

Do you have nerves of steel, the patience of Job, and an unending sense of humor? If so, your lot in life may be as a *driver-training instructor*—you have the perfect qualifications.

The first requirement of becoming a driver-training instructor is that you must be a qualified driver yourself. This means that you must have a satisfactory driving record, free of excessive violations. The next step, in most states, is to become licensed or certified. If you plan to become hired to teach in a public school driver-training program, it is required to get the job. If you plan to offer private lessons, it is necessary, since your teen-age students will need to take certified or approved lessons in order to receive a decrease in their auto insurance rates for having taken driver training.

Licensing requirements vary from state to state, and you should check with your State Department of Transportation for specifics. Often, it is necessary to take a driver-training instruction program to become certified.

Once you are certified, you can offer your services in a number of ways. Perhaps the easiest is to teach for someone else, since you will have no investment in vehicles, materials, or operating expenses. Public schools offering driver-training lessons and private driver-training schools are obvious contacts that you should make. Most often, you will be paid a generous hourly wage, at perhaps three to five times the minimum wage rate.

Another possibility is to offer your own private driver-training instruction. Here again, before starting, you should check with your State Department of Transportation or Department of Education to determine what is necessary to start a licensed driver-training school. Your basic equipment will be a good vehicle, in excellent repair, which is outfitted with dual controls (an extra brake pedal installed on the passenger side). You will also need space suitable for classroom instruction.

Ordinarily, your activities will include several hours of classroom instruction before the student begins to drive. You will teach, or review, driving regulations, laws, and procedures. The majority of your driver-training program will consist of behind-the-wheel instruction. Here, you will teach everything the student will need to know to become a competent driver and to pass their driver's license exam.

You can offer students a program, consisting of a set number of lessons, or you can offer a flexible arrangement where the student takes only as many lessons as are necessary to become competent. A certain number of hours of instruction may be prescribed in your state for teen-age students, and you should become familiar with those requirements.

There are many potential students for your driver-training lessons. These include unlicensed teen-agers whose school does not offer driver-training, teen-agers who prefer private lessons to school-offered group lessons, and teen-agers who need additional training beyond that offered at their school. Also, the elderly, adults who have never learned to drive, and persons moving into your state are good possibilities.

In addition to offering instruction on how to drive an automobile, you might expand your instruction to *chauffeur training* and *motorcycle driver training*.

If you operate your own driver-training school, you will incur expenses for increased insurance coverage (make sure you check with your agent), automobile operating expenses, automobile depreciation, and miscellaneous books and materials. The tuition you charge should cover all these costs in addition to paying you a substantial hourly wage of perhaps three to five times the minimum wage rate.

When selecting a vehicle to use for your driver-training lessons, check with your local automobile dealers to see if any of them or their companies offer a special program to furnish automobiles to driver-training schools. This is sometimes done as a form of advertising, with the idea in mind that student drivers will become impressed with the brand and later buy one for themselves.

Promote your driver-training lessons by advertising in the telephone directory yellow pages and in classified ads in local newspapers. You might also contact school counselors and make your service known to driver's license examiners.

In addition to earning good money on a part-time basis, teaching driver training offers the additional bonus of being able to witness the fruits of your labor as students make steady progress. This, and helping people reach a goal, can be very satisfying.

Fund Raiser

*F*UND RAISER—sounds interesting, you say, but probably a pretty limited field, not much opportunity. This might be your first reaction, but if you stop to think about it, there are hundreds of thousands of organizations that exist on donated funds. You are probably contacted by a dozen or more yourself each year. In fact, fund raising is one of the *biggest* industries in the country.

Those who rely upon donated funds entirely or partially include churches, colleges, charities, political organizations, museums, hospitals, research foundations, and centers for the mentally retarded, emotionally disturbed, handicapped, and orphaned. The list could go on and on, and you can probably identify many of them in your own community by name.

Some specific purposes for which you might perform fundraising activities include a new library for a college, a cathederal for a religious organization, or a civic center for a city. Perhaps you will help establish or enlarge a college or church endowment fund. On the other hand, the goal may be to secure funds for normal day-to-day operations.

Your primary function as a fund raiser is to encourage individuals and businesses to donate money to the worthwhile cause you are promoting. This involves several different types and levels of activity. Often, the work is almost entirely organizational. You publicize the organization's need for funds and the beneficial use that will be made of the donations. This might involve development of printed literature and news releases and the organization of special fund-raising activities like concerts, raffles, telethons, bike-a-thons, $100- or $1,000-a-plate dinners, or dance-a-thons.

The fund-raising work force for many organizations consists of a staff that is paid, one of whom is you, and a score of unpaid but concerned volunteers. A major part of your activities, then, may involve recruiting, training, and supervising volunteers.

Once the fund-raising plans have been made, they must be carried out. You will need to keep volunteers' interest high and must maintain accurate records so you can monitor the program's success.

Qualifications and skills needed to be successful at this level of fund raising include organizational ability, creativity, thorough follow-up, and the ability to get along with people and to supervise their activities.

Another type of fund-raising activity is that of making personal contacts with potential major contributors. In this role, you are a salesperson. You first conduct research to determine who might be inclined to have a vested interest in the proposition you are promoting. Often, these potential donors are easy to identify—they are alumni of the college, present or former members of the church or association, former recipients of the organization's services, or simply community-minded or concerned people and businesses. You will contact them in person, explain your organization's plans and needs, and solicit a contribution.

Since you may be seeking donations in the thousands of dollars, each potential donor may receive cautious courting over an extended time period. Often, this class of potential donor is beleaguered by numerous requests for donations from all sorts of organizations. Therefore, you must do a good selling job to convince them of the good they can do and of the satisfactions they will receive by supporting your cause.

Special qualifications are necessary to be successful at this level of fund raising. Since you will most likely be dealing with well-moneyed people and business executives, you must feel at ease with this class of clientele. Conversational ability, thorough knowledge of tax laws pertaining to advantages of making donations, and a professional manner are necessities. Full-time fund raisers of this type often travel the entire country to make their contacts. Since you will work on a part-time basis, your contacts will be limited to an accessible local geographic area.

It is possible to moonlight as a fund raiser in a number of different ways. One is to become an employee of a professional fund-raising company that serves a variety of clients. Another is to work for a specific organization, like a college or major charity, that has its own fund-raising staff. Since many fund-raising projects have a peak season of increased activity, part-time temporary employment is often available.

A third possibility is to offer your own fund-raising service where you serve smaller clients who cannot afford or do not need a full-time fund raiser. Included in this category are those who need to raise funds for a special project like a new structure or to establish an endowment fund. Here, your activities might be as a consultant, or you might help organize the entire plan of action and perhaps even get involved in direct solicitation of funds.

Virtually no investment in equipment or materials is required to become a fund raiser, since you are offering a service. No specific educational requirements exist, but a background in public relations, advertising, accounting, and income taxes will be impressive to many employers and clients.

Potential income for a part-time fund raiser can vary a great deal depending upon the level at which you enter this profession. If you are an employee of a professional fund-raising company or of a specific organization, you may be paid an hourly wage. As you demonstrate your ability to devise, organize, and supervise fund-raising activities that work, your income will rise. If you operate your own fund-raising service, the income potential can be great. Ordinarily, a specific fund-raising project is bid at a flat amount, based on a handsome hourly rate for your services.

Besides offering good earnings potential, moonlighting as a fund raiser can be an exciting and action-packed experience that offers the added satisfaction of helping a nonprofit organization accomplish its worthwhile goals for the good of many people.

Related fields of employment worth considering include *public relations, promotions,* and being a *lobbyist.*

Government Employee

Do YOU know who is the nation's largest employer? Well, it is the government, and you can join the crowd by moonlighting as a *government employee.*

Perhaps it should first be clarified just what is meant by "the government." Actually, that term involves a lot of territoy, including city, county, state, and federal governmental units, and encompassing administrative agencies, public schools, and public universities. But do government units actually hire part-time employees? The answer is yes—at every level. The U.S. Congress has passed the Federal Employee's Part-Time Career Employment Act, which requires federal government agencies to establish and expand part-time employment opportunities. Thus, with the federal government leading the way, more possibilities to moonlight at all levels of government exist than ever before.

At the city level, opportunities may exist with the fire, police, or street maintenance departments. The recreation department can often use additional instructors and supervisors for children's sports and games during the summer months and for adult programs of all types year round. The city park department, particularly in the spring and summer, often needs help to groom and maintain lawns, trees, shrubs, and flower gardens. Also, on the city level, it is possible to work as a part-time *building code inspector* or *fire code inspector,* where you would determine if city regulations are being followed in new construction projects and in existing structures as well.

Since the city library is open in the range of 12 to 15 hours or more each day, it also holds excellent part-time work potential for you as a *library clerk*. Then too, the various offices in City Hall should not be overlooked.

On the county level, you might consider becoming the *disaster preparedness director* (formerly called *civil defense director*), which might occupy several hours per day year round, or the *weed commissioner*, which is seasonal in many parts of the country. Perhaps you would enjoy being a *bailiff*, who performs miscellaneous duties while court is in session. In a similar area, the positions of *magistrate* or *justice of the peace* are often occupied part-time by people with little or no previous legal training. The county assessor's office usually hires part-time help during the assessment period when property owners sign up for their homestead exemptions and declare their personal property. Often, the county maintenance department can use additional help, particularly for summer road maintenance and during the winter snow-removal season.

The county extension office, county fair board, welfare department, social services department, veterans affairs commission, zoning office, and other departments and offices are also worth contacting. If you have a flair for politics, you might even seek election to the *county board of supervisors*, which can be an interesting and prestigious position as well as a good-paying one.

Numerous state offices, departments, and divisions provide employment possibilities at both the state capitol and at locations throughout the state. Some areas that might be particularly appealing include those in agriculture, commerce, conservation, public safety, health, public instruction, and social services. You can work as an employee; or, if you are particularly knowledgeable or interested in some area, you might actively seek appointment to a board or commission.

The federal government offers the widest range of employment possibilities of any governmental unit. One of the most appealing part-time jobs is with the U.S. Postal Department, where positions as *postal clerk, mail handler, city mail carrier, rural mail carrier,* and others are often available. The Small Business Administration, military services, and Departments of Transportation, Agriculture, Health, Internal Revenue, Interior, and others also offer good possibilities.

Opportunities with a public school system include *teacher's aide, food service employee, playground supervisor,* or *study hall monitor.* Colleges and universities often hire part-timers to work in the library or with food service or to supervise student housing. Also, custodial, security, and maintenance positions are often available. Another possibility is to work directly for teachers at any level of education from first grade through graduate school— as a *homework paper checker.* Here, you would relieve teachers of one of their most time-consuming tasks—checking homework and perhaps test papers as well.

The general procedure for obtaining a job as a government employee is the same as securing any other type of job—you apply for it. On the city, county, and state levels, civil service exams may or may not be administered, depending upon the type of position and the governmental unit's procedures. Written exams are usually administered for clerical or office positions. Oral or practical-application exams might be administered for those jobs requiring special skill or knowledge or those that involve manual labor. In some cases, no exams are administered, and the evaluation is based on the applicant's education, background, and experience.

Often, cities, counties, and states require that the applicant be a resident of that particular jurisdiction to be eligible for the position.

Most applicants for a federal government position must pass a civil service exam, which is usually written. However, the "job element approach" is used in evaluating applicants for some manual-labor positions. Here, a task list is developed of specific activities that would be performed on the job. The applicants then identify the tasks they are capable of performing. In addition to the testing procedures, personal interviews are also employed in evaluating applicants. For upper-level positions, the applicant's experience, education, background, and the results of personal interviews are used exclusively as the evaluation process.

Exams for federal government positions are administered by the U.S. Office of Personnel Management through hundreds of local Federal Job Information Centers throughout the country. Your nearest testing center can be located by checking under *United States Government* in your telephone directory.

Usually, part-time government employees, especially those at the state and federal levels, receive the regular pay rate for that job. A pro rata amount of fringe benefits is also usually received.

Government jobs are generally known to provide a comfortable work environment, satisfactory pay rate, acceptable fringe benefits, and solid job security. Therefore, working for the nation's largest employer may be the perfect way to moonlight.

Guide—Hunting and Fishing

Do you know where the hot spots are? The hot spots for hunting and fishing, that is. If so, you can pursue your favorite hobby and earn good money at the same time, as a *hunting or fishing guide.*

The main requirements to become a hunting or fishing guide are simple—you must know where the fish are biting or where game can be bagged. This means you need to be thoroughly familiar with the characteristics and habits of the fish or game you are pursuing. You need to know how weather conditions, time of day, and other factors will influence their behavior. Besides understanding the prey, you must know the habitat. Where in the lake, stream, forest, field, or mountain is the best place to fish or hunt? In addition, you need to know what type of gear or equipment is most suitable to use.

To be a successful guide, it is helpful to have additional skills beyond the technical knowledge. Since your clients are people, human relations skills are necessary. You will need to convince your clients to do things the right way—your way, to follow certain rules and regulations, and to stay within legal and ethical limits. Organizational skills are also necessary, since you may often guide a group of people and will need to direct everyone's activities to avoid confusion and conflict. Then too, a basic understanding of business principles and practices is helpful, since being a guide is, in reality, being a businessperson.

When you are convinced that you possess the necessary technical knowledge, human relations skills, organizational abilities, and business sense, you are ready to begin. You can be an independent guide, making all your own contacts with clients, or you can become an employee of a bait and tackle shop or hunting lodge.

If you are an employee, the employer will organize the hunting and fishing expeditions and you will perform all the activities from that point onward. You will receive an hourly wage or a set amount per expedition.

If you are an independent guide, you will need to develop your own clientele. Many customers will result from personal contacts made on your own hunting or fishing expeditions. You can also advertise in local publications and in hunting or fishing guides. Make contacts with bait and tackle shops, hunting lodges, sporting goods stores, hotels, motels, campgrounds, bars, restaurants, and other businesses in your hunting or fishing area. Leave business cards and ask the business operator to pass them on to hunters and fishers with whom they come in contact.

Secure the names and address of all clients for whom you provide your guide services. Many of these people will return to your area for subsequent fishing or hunting expeditions, and if you keep in touch with them, they will undoubtedly use your services again. Consider mailing them a periodic newsletter with reports on hunting or fishing activities, or at least contact them during the time of year when hunting or fishing expeditions are being planned.

Your investment may be small or it may be substantial, depending upon the nature of your guide business and how you approach it. If you require your clients to furnish all of their own gear and equipment, you will need to provide only your personal services and your knowledge. On the other hand, you might provide boats, horses, four-wheel drive vehicles, or whatever else your clients need. You will, of course, include the use of these items in your fee or charge an extra rental amount for them. You might also provide bait, food, beverages, and so on.

Set your fee at an hourly rate or at a flat amount per expedition. You might charge per person, or you can limit the group to a certain number and charge a group rate.

Moonlighting as a hunting or fishing guide can be a great seasonal or weekend activity. You might develop expert knowledge in several different areas, though, so you can provide a guide service virtually year round.

You might also consider operating a *hunting lodge,* where you provide a complete package of hunting services for your clients, including lodging, meals, and your guide service.

Another possibility is to operate a *fishing pond,* where you would stock a private pond with trout, bass, or other popular fish and sell admittance allowing people to fish there. If you own the right type of land in a hunting area, you can follow the same principle to establish a *hunting refuge.* Here, you would declare the land off limits to all but those who pay you a fee to hunt there.

Handyman Service

ARE YOU a tinkerer? Are you good at fixing leaky water pipes, patching nail holes in walls, putting on storm windows, and installing curtain rods? If so, you are able to do what many others cannot do, or will not do, and you have the perfect moonlighting opportunity right in your own hands—you can operate a *handyman service*.

As a handyman, you will do just as the title suggests. You will do whatever odd jobs someone needs to have done. This might include all sorts of miscellaneous household repair work like replacing a broken windowpane, repairing a cracked wall or ceiling, or replacing a broken doorknob. In addition, you can do installations like hanging a mirror or a door or building shelves in a storage area. You might provide a cleanup service where you clean ovens or refrigerators or clean out an attic. You might even offer a delivery service where you haul large items like old furniture or mattresses to the dump grounds or refuse collection center, or where you haul larger appliances like television sets to the repair shop.

You can offer all these services or you might specialize in only one area. Obviously, the more diverse your offerings, the more opportunity you will have to be of good service to your customers and, of course, to increase your income.

Potential customers will include the elderly, people who are too busy to do their own odd jobs, and those who are unfamiliar with making repairs or are afraid to tackle the job. Also, real estate offices (who often have responsibility for the care of vacant houses) and lending institutions (who often have vacant repossessions) should not be overlooked. In other words, there are *lots* of potential customers.

The necessary equipment will vary with the services you offer, but a good assortment of hand tools and a few basic electric tools should be sufficient. You should also carry a well-stocked chest of nails, screws, bolts, glues, patching plaster, electrical tape, cleansers, touch-up paint, and other commonly used hardware and supplies. You should be equipped well enough so that you can make most repairs and installations on the spot without needing to drive to a store for materials.

Success in this business venture will depend upon the quality of your work, your attitude and demeanor in dealing with customers, and the prices you charge. Since many elderly people and single women, who will compose a significant portion of your customers, are leery of being taken advantage of by unscrupulous operators, you should take extra precautions to exude sincerity and honesty. Do only that work which is necessary, but at the same time, look for and point out other potential problems that may require attention in the near future.

If you treat your customers honestly, fairly, and respectfully, and charge a reasonable fee, you will build a steady following of happy, loyal customers who will call upon you time after time. This is one of the main keys to your success.

In most cases, you will be able to set your own hours and work by appointment as it best fits into your schedule. Be prepared, however, for an occasional emergency call that will require immediate attention.

Charge an hourly rate or a set amount per job. Probably, your rate will not match that of an electrician or plumber, but you will be able to earn an outstanding part-time income, nevertheless. A charge of two to four times the minimum wage rate might be easily obtainable, depending upon your geographic location.

A handyman service may be the ideal moonlighting activity for the person who likes variety. Certainly, no two jobs will be exactly the same. It is also a great way to meet many wonderful people and to help others who are in need of assistance.

If your handyman service grows to the point where you have more customers than you can handle, you might consider hiring one or more competent and trustworthy helpers.

Hauling Service

THE BASIC fact that there are more people who need things hauled than there are people who have trucks gives rise to a good moonlighting opportunity—operating a *hauling service*.

The nature of a hauling service is simple: you haul things for other people. What type of things? Just about anything.

The *moving business* is one good possibility—not long-distance hauling, perhaps, but short-distance hauling. In other words, you might specialize in moving people's goods from one house or apartment in the community to another. You can provide only your truck and your own labor, or you can round up a crew of moonlighting friends to help and you can offer a full-fledged moving service. This service will appeal to just about anyone, but single women (who ordinarily don't own trucks and who may not want to lug furniture), college students, and the elderly may find it particularly attractive.

Exercise particular care so that you do not damage your customers' property. Wrap furniture and appliances in blankets and pack breakable items in sturdy boxes with proper insulation.

Set your rate to include an hourly wage for each worker and to cover your vehicle's operating expenses. You can pay each worker somewhat less than the hourly rate received from your customer, thus earning a management fee for organizing the job. Another possibility is to bid each job at a flat amount. You will need to estimate carefully the amount of time required so that you do not end up working at a substandard wage or charging your customers an excessive amount.

A *garbage hauling service* can also be considered if you live in a community where independent haulers are permitted to operate. With this business, you will establish a regular route, picking up garbage from each customer once or twice per week.

Set your charge at a certain amount per pickup, per week, or per month. You might offer your customers the option of having garbage picked up either once or twice per week, with a different charge for each type of service.

A profitable side benefit of operating a garbage hauling service is that you can salvage many usable and salable items from what others have thrown away.

A *commercial hauling service* is another possibility. Here, you will deliver furniture, appliances, pianos, or other large items for local businesses. Most likely, any business that has a large volume in these products will have its own delivery fleet. Therefore, it is the smaller dealer or part-time dealer that might best be able to use your services. Upholstery shops, secondhand stores, and appliance repair shops might be ideal customers. Large dealers should not be overlooked, however, since they may need extra help during peak seasonal periods or when special sales are run.

Set your rate at a flat amount per delivery plus mileage for use of your vehicle, or charge by the hour.

Contractors, roofers, and others in the building trades might also be able to use your hauling service. When they complete a job, they are usually anxious to get on to the next one. Often, they are too busy to properly clean up the construction site, or it is not economical to have their highly paid workers do it. Therefore, they might contract with you, for a flat amount, to clean up the area and to haul the debris away. Actually, *debris* is not a totally accurate term to use here, since usable and salable wood and metals will often be among the spoils. Set your rate based on an estimate of your time involved and your operating expenses.

In addition to the specific possibilities previously mentioned, you can offer a *free-lance hauling service*. You would offer to haul anything for anybody at any time. This might include hauling a television set or appliance to a repair shop, hauling furniture to an upholsterer, or picking up a load of firewood. You might also haul away fallen tree limbs, yard leaves, and unwanted large household items like furniture and appliances. You can charge a flat fee per job, based upon a careful estimate of your time invested and your operating expenses.

Regardless of the type of hauling service you operate, you should first check to see if a special permit or license is required. If you do local hauling only, a license or permit through the city clerk's office or county recorder's office will probably be sufficient, if required at all. If you do long-distance hauling, licensing through the State Department of Transportation may be necessary. Also check with your insurance agent, since additional coverage will probably be necessary because you will be using your vehicle for hire.

About the only equipment you will need to operate your hauling service is your truck—that and a strong back. Almost any size truck can be used for most types of hauling, including the mini-size ones. Depending on the nature of your service, specialized equipment, like a dolly, may also be helpful.

Operating a hauling service is an excellent way to earn part-time income for yourself and to put family members and friends to work as well. You can regulate your time and income by the number of customers you accept and can always expand the business by hiring more people and trucks to work for you.

If you like the idea of hauling things for people but don't have a truck, you might operate a *delivery service.* You would use your automobile to make deliveries for florists, pharmacies, supermarkets, and others who deal in smaller-sized products.

Home Product Sales

Wouldn't it be convenient if retailers came to your home with their products rather than your having to go to them? Many people would answer that question with an enthusiastic yes. Well, you can provide that convenience by becoming involved in *home product sales*.

Many products, including cologne, cleaners, cosmetics, jewelry, cooking utensils, cutlery, food supplements, and other household and personal-use products are sold by company representatives who call on their customers in their homes. Sales are made by calling on customers one at a time or through the use of the home party plan.

If sales are made to customers on an individual basis, you might develop an established route that you service at regular intervals, say monthly. You demonstrate samples of the products and display other items in your company-furnished catalog. You take orders and submit them to your company. The company ships the goods to you, and you deliver them when you make your next visit. Products like cosmetics and food supplements, which are used on a regular basis, are ideal for this sales technique.

At first, you will need to prospect for customers by contacting acquaintances, using referrals, and perhaps making cold calls door to door. Once you have developed regular customers, your work becomes easier, since your main activity then is to service your established accounts.

Other products, like cooking utensils and cutlery, have a long life and are therefore purchased infrequently. In this situation, your sales technique is to prospect for suitable customers, make appointments, and demonstrate your product. You might demonstrate to one prospect at a time or you might ask your prospects to invite one or more friends for a group presentation.

Your presentation may be lengthy, perhaps lasting one or two hours. An important part of it will be the demonstration. For example, if you are selling cooking utensils, you might cook dinner for your prospect, using your product.

Your customers for this type of product will buy from you infrequently, perhaps only once in a lifetime. Therefore, a major part of your sales activity is to continually prospect for customers.

A third type of sales technique is the *home party plan*. Under this arrangement, you will ask a prospect to act as a home party host or hostess. This person will invite a group of perhaps 10 to 20 friends to their home to view your products. You will display the goods, demonstrate them, provide an evening of lively entertainment, and take orders. In return for doing the prospecting for you and for hosting the party, the host or hostess will receive gifts of products from you, based on the sales volume generated at the party. Your company will ship the products to you, and you will deliver them to the buyers.

This sales technique is ideal for household products such as plastic containers or interior decorator items or for personal items like jewelry, wigs, or cosmetics.

Many items suitable for home product sales can be sold via two, or perhaps all three, of the preceding sales techniques. The nature of the product, your company's directives, and your own preference will decide which is best.

Your primary role is that of a salesperson, although your company may give you a fancier title such as consultant, fashion coordinator, distributor, or manager. Nevertheless, the most important of your activities will be prospecting for new customers and serving your established accounts.

Ordinarily, your income is based on a percentage of sales, which often amounts to 25 to 40 percent of the sales price. Therefore, if you can develop steady sales for lower-priced products, or sell a few higher-priced ones, your income can easily amount to several hundred dollars per month on a part-time basis.

With many companies, you can recruit other salespeople to sell beneath you in the organizational structure and receive a commission override on their sales. In some companies, this is possible only after you have demonstrated successful sales results over an extended time period and are officially promoted within the company. In multilevel sales organizations like Amway or

Shakley, however, you can virtually begin building your sales organization right away.

With some companies, the home product salespeople must buy their own demonstration kit of products. With others, the kit is provided on a loan basis, with perhaps a minimal deposit required. In still other cases, sales are made almost exclusively from the company's catalog. Other than this possible cost for securing demonstration materials, there is usually no investment required, except for a vehicle for making sales contacts and deliveries.

Home product sales can be an exciting, fun, and profitable way to moonlight. You will meet many interesting people and will be able to purchase many useful products at a discount. Also, many of these companies have sales contests whereby you can earn cash bonuses or even free vacations.

The following companies manufacture or distribute goods for home product sales. You may wish to contact one or more of them for specific information.

Amway Corporation (Household products, cleaners, etc.)
7575 East Fulton Road
Ada, MI 49355

Avon Products, Inc. (Cosmetics)
9 West 57th Street
New York, NY 10019

Cameo Manufacturing Company, Inc. (Jewelry)
45 Richmond Street
Providence, RI 02903

Sarah Coventry, Inc. (Jewelry)
Sarah Coventry Parkway
Newark, NY 14513

Mary Kaye Cosmetics, Inc. (Makeup, colognes)
8900 John W. Carpenter Freeway
Dallas, TX 75247

Shakley Corporation (Food supplements, cosmetics,
    cleaners)
1900 Powell Street
Everyville, CA 94608

Stanley Home Products, Inc. (Brushes, household and
    industrial chemicals)
333 Western Avenue
Westfield, MA 01085

Tupperwear (Plastic household products)
Drawer D
Woonsocket, RI 02895

Wear-ever Aluminum, Inc. (Cooking utensils and cutlery)
1089 Eastern Avenue
Chillicothe, OH 45601

Hypnotist

How would you like to learn an activity that can be
used in criminal investigations, business training, personal heatlh
improvement, mental health treatment, weight loss, and entertainment—and which has dozens of other uses as well? Where
people are in awe of your abilities and mystified by your feats?
Where you can charge fees that are comparable to those of
accountants, lawyers, or dentists? And that is so easy to enter
that there are generally no educational requirements, licenses,
or permits? Sound too good to be true? Well, it *is* true—and it
can all come true for you too, if you decide to moonlight as a
hypnotist.

You are probably aware of some of the uses of hypnotism
but may not be familiar with all its applications. In fact, probably

no one understands the full potential that exists for applying hypnosis, since it is still an emerging and evolving field.

One of the most familiar uses of hypnotism is for entertainment. Here, a group of people is brought on stage and told that their pants are on fire or that they have just inherited a million dollars or that they are driving a high-speed sports car whose brakes have just failed while descending a winding, mountain highway. All the while, observers roll in the aisles with laughter as they watch the hypnotized subjects go through their paces.

In criminal investigations, eyewitnesses are often hypnotized to increase their recall of events. In mental health treatment, patients are hypnotized to seek out some deep-seated problem or long-forgotten event. Hypnotism is used to develop and increase the self-esteem, confidence, and determination of people in business and sales. It is used to increase the concentration, relaxation, and performance of athletes.

Then too, one of hypnotism's best-known uses is to help individuals lose weight, stop smoking, stop biting their fingernails, increase their sexual prowess, or modify their behavior in some other way.

Hypnotism can be an ideal activity to be combined with an existing job or for moonlighting in a closely related area. For instance, it is a natural for people in law enforcement and the criminal investigation field, psychologists, psychiatrists, and others in the mental health area, athletic trainers, and those in the field of sales training.

How about training and certification? One would probably think that years of training are required and that a person must be a psychologist, psychiatrist, or both, in order to become a hypnotist—right? Well, nothing could be further from the truth. Probably the reason that people think intensive training is required is that a hypnotist works with a person's mind. It is therefore assumed that an amateur hypnotist might put someone into a trance and never be able to bring them back out or might somehow damage a person's mind by not handling the hypnotized person in some prescribed manner. Probably the antics of show business hypnotists have done much to foster these ideas—these misconceptions.

Actually, authorities report that hypnosis is absolutely harmless and that there has never been a reported case of anyone ever being injured or adversely affected by it in any way. As far as someone being put into a hypnotic trance from which they cannot be waken—well, if that did happen, the subject would simply sleep it off and awake in a few hours as good as new or maybe even better from the experience. Most likely, however, this eventuality would never even happen.

This harmless nature of hypnosis is reflected in the training requirements, licensing, and certification of hypnotists in each state. Generally, there are no requirements whatsoever. In most states, you can simply hang up a shingle and go to work.

Obviously, however, in order to know how to perform hypnosis, to be able to convince clients that you know what you're doing, and to get results, you will need some type of training. It is also suggested, since the field of hypnosis is evolving and growing, that you check with your State Department of Health to determine if, by chance, any recent certification requirements have been instituted.

Training in hypnosis can be received in one of four basic ways. One is to align yourself with a practicing hypnotist who will teach you what you need to know. Most likely, this opportunity will be available only if you plan to join that hypnotist as an associate or if you pay handsomely for the instruction.

The other three methods of learning hypnosis involve taking courses at an established hypnosis institute or school. The differences lies in the type of training program, the program's length, and its intensity. One type of program provides intensive training over an extended period, say nine months. A second type offers concentrated study of perhaps 100 hours in a two-week period. The third method consists of a weekend seminar or a series of two or three weekend seminars. Three well-established hypnosis institutions that you may wish to contact are: Hypnosis Institute, Colleyville, TX 76034; Hypnosis Training Institute of Los Angeles, 312 Riverdale Drive, Glendale, CA 91204; and Ethical Hypnosis Training Center, 60 Vose Avenue, South Orange, NJ 07079.

Most attempts at granting certification or of setting standards and requirements for hypnotists are undertaken by the various national hypnosis associations. These are groups to which members belong voluntarily, and some of them function in close association with hypnosis training schools. One of these associations, the American Council of Hypnotist Examiners, certifies applicants in all 50 states and bestows the designations of *hypnotist, master hypnotist,* or *hypnotherapist* upon persons meeting certain requirements.

Once you have learned how to perform hypnosis, you are ready to begin offering your services in one or more of the ways previously described. If you specialize mainly in working with individuals, you can operate out of your home or set up a separate clinic in a small office area. If you plan to work with business clients or perform your services for those in law enforcement or the health care areas, you should ideally also develop some knowledge in those specialized subjects. That is so you will understand the relevant needs, problems, and goals.

The rates you can charge for performing your services can be almost overwhelming. Amounts at 5 to 20 times the minimum wage rate per hour are common, and even more is charged by some hypnotists. Primarily, your reputation for successful results will determine what clients will find to be a palatable amount. Your appearance, manner, style, and showmanship will also be factors that will build your client's confidence in you. Also, the way you package your sessions will affect your earnings. For instance, you might specialize in one-time weight-loss and stop-smoking treatments (often ineffective), or you might set up a program of 3 to 10 visits. If you advertise and promote your service well, you can undoubtedly be as busy as you want to be and can easily earn hundreds of dollars per week on a part-time basis.

If moonlighting as a hypnotist sounds interesting to you, it is suggested that you sit down in a comfortable chair, fold your hands limply in your lap, relax every muscle in your body, fix your eyes on an imaginary spot on the ceiling, and concentrate on becoming a hypnotist while I count backward from ten. Ready? Relax now—10, 9, 8, 7, 6, 5, 4, 3, 2, 1 . . .

Independent Contractor

IF YOU'RE the type of person who likes to tackle a job, work on it using your own methods without having constant supervision, and be judged only on your finished product, you might consider moonlighting as an *independent contractor.*

The first step to becoming an independent contractor is to choose an area in which you have knowledge and skill or in which you can develop these abilities. This can be done by gaining practical experience by working with others, learning on your own by completing projects for your own use, or by taking a part-time or full-time course from a vocational-technical school or specialized institute.

Carpentry, dock installation and removal, weatherproofing, fireplace installation, insulating, fence installation, plumbing, swimming-pool cleaning, and glass installation are all areas worth considering. Others include becoming a sign hanger, plasterer, tree- and stump-removal contractor, dry-wall installer, dry-wall taperer, or cement contractor. You might contract to process mailings for a company or handle some other special project for a business or office. Just about anything can be suitable.

An advantage you have as a part-time independent contractor is that you can specialize in one phase of your business rather than attempting to handle all types of jobs. This allows you to control and limit your investment in equipment and the amount of knowledge required. For example, if you are a cement contractor, you can specialize in installing sidewalks or home driveways only. By specializing in one or two areas, you can learn to do your work with extreme competency and efficiency, thus improving your chances of landing almost any job that comes along in your area.

In some cases, you may be able to perform all of the work yourself, while in others, a two- or three-person crew at a minimum may be necessary.

The amount of equipment needed and investment required will vary a great deal with the type of work you do and your scope of operation. Ordinarily, if a large investment is required, your rates will be set accordingly to deliver a satisfactory return on your investment.

In all cases, you should secure adequate liability insurance to protect yourself against claims for damages to a customer's property, or for any personal injuries caused by you or your work. You should also check with the city clerk and county recorder to determine if any licenses or permits are required to operate your business. Often, they are not, but if they are needed, they are usually easy and inexpensive to obtain. Also, you should become familiar with any building code regulations that pertain to your area of work and you should complete all jobs within those guidelines.

As a small independent contractor, you may need to seek out customers, at least in the beginning. In addition to normal advertising and promotional techniques, you should contact large general contractors who might sublet smaller jobs to you. Also, be alert to ways you can use a direct sales approach to stimulate business. For example, if you sell and install insulation, you can go door to door and offer to make a free survey of the home's current insulation status or energy efficiency level. No doubt, your free service will divulge that many homes are underinsulated, and you will have located potential customers.

Often, independent contractors are asked to *bid* a job. This means that you make an offer at a specific price for which you will do the work. If your bid is accepted, that amount becomes the contract price. Sometimes the bid will be for labor only, while in other cases the bid will include all materials, supplies, and labor to provide a finished product.

Great care and skill must be exercised in making a bid. If you build in too high a profit margin, someone else will probably underbid you, and you will lose the job. If you bid too low, you may get the job but earn no profit for doing it. This is the tightrope that is walked by the independent contractor. Often, a very satisfactory, if not handsome, profit can be earned from bid jobs if you work more efficiently and quickly than the time allotment upon which your bid was based.

On the other hand, many jobs are not secured on the bid basis. Instead, you will be hired to do the job and will be paid an hourly wage. This can also be profitable since you will be paid at perhaps two to six times the minimum wage rate for yourself and any helpers. You will, of course, pay helpers less than you charge your customers per hour, thus receiving an override for organizing the job, providing equipment, and accepting responsibility for the finished product.

In addition, any materials provided by you will be billed to your customers at regular retail prices. Since you are a contractor, you will receive a discount of perhaps 15 to 20 percent on these items from your suppliers and thus make an additional profit here. If you want, of course, you can pass all or part of these discounts along to your customers.

Regardless of whether you bid jobs or are paid by the hour, your hourly rate will be the basis of your income. Since you can probably operate out of your home or from a small, inexpensive location, you can afford to charge lower rates than many competitors, if you want, but still maintain a similar level of profit.

If you are highly specialized in what you do, you can probably even charge more than your competitors, since customers are almost always willing to pay a little extra for a high-quality job.

Two types of independent contractors that merit special mention are *house painters* and *wallpaper hangers.* This is because of the huge potential that exists and because almost everyone possesses, or can easily develop, the basic skills necessary to enter these two areas. Also, a relatively small investment is required.

Little, if any, actual training is necessary to become a house painter. You can paint exteriors, interiors, or both, thereby having the potential to keep busy year round. In addition to painting houses, good possibilities exist to paint apartment buildings, businesses, schools, office buildings, and farm buildings.

The primary qualifications needed for house painting are that you be conscientious, thorough, reliable, and fastidious. Since you are billing yourself as a professional painter, your finished jobs must look as though they were completed by a professional. Knowledge of which paints and stains are appropriate to use in any given situation and of the best methods of applying them by brush, roller, sponge, or sprayer is also necessary. This can easily be learned in a short time by talking to suppliers of paint and painting materials.

The cost of establishing your house-painting business can be low, particularly if you specialize in interiors only. Basic equipment will include a variety of brushes, rollers, trays, scrapers, and drop cloths. One or more stepladders is also necessary. If you do exterior painting, an extension ladder and scaffolding may be mandatory. A paint sprayer and air compressor may be a worthwhile investment, particularly if you stain rough-sawn exteriors or paint barns, sheds, or other outbuildings.

If you develop skill in using your paint sprayer, you might also specialize in *automobile painting* or *parking-lot striping.*

The obvious activity of a wallpaper hanger is to cover walls, and perhaps ceilings, with wallpaper, fabric, vinyl, or some other material. Other activities can include moving furniture out of the room or covering it with a drop cloth and preparing the wall surface. This might involve removing layers of old wallpaper by steaming or scraping and then patching cracks and nail holes.

Equipment needed to become a wallpaper hanger includes a portable table for rolling out the wallpaper and applying paste, a stepladder, and a variety of brushes, rollers, and knives. This requires a relatively small investment, a few hundred dollars at most. If you accept jobs in areas with high ceilings, such as entryways and lobbies, you will probably need scaffolding since it may be too time consuming and dangerous to work from a ladder.

Wallpaper hanging can be learned in a number of ways. One is to practice on your own by papering your own walls and volunteering to do those of friends and relatives until you become confident enough to market your skills. Another is to work with an experienced wallpaper hanger as a helper. If your goal is to become a well-trained professional, you can attend a 10-week course offered by the United States School of Professional Paperhanging, 16 Chaplin Avenue, Rutland, VT 05701.

Three factors that make becoming an independent contractor an attractive way to moonlight are the independence, the income potential, and the growth potential. It is one of the moonlighting activities that most often develops into a successful full-time career.

Insurance Claim Adjuster

THE FACT that one unfortunate event could financially wipe out most people and many companies gives rise to one of the biggest businesses in the world—the insurance industry. The fact that occasionally these unfortunate events do occur, and that insurance companies must make payment, gives

rise to a moonlighting possibility within the insurance industry—
that of *insurance claim adjuster.*

As an insurance claim adjuster, you would analyze the loss
suffered by a policyholder and make a determination of the
amount of money the policyholder should receive or of what
other adjustment should be made. You would work for either a
specific insurance company or for an independent adjusting
company that handles claim adjustments on a free-lance basis
for any number of insurance companies. In either case, your
duties would be basically the same.

One type of claim-adjusting opportunity that is available on
a seasonal basis is as a *crop hail adjuster.* The season begins as
soon as the crop comes up out of the ground and ends when
the crop is harvested. During this period, you might work full
time or part time. It is often the ideal moonlighting opportunity
for teachers who receive a lengthy summer vacation, semiretired
persons, or farmers who do not raise livestock.

Many companies have recently expanded their coverage to
multiperil crop insurance, which covers drought, drowning, wind,
hail, and any other type of damage. Therefore, more employment opportunity than ever now exists in this area, since there
is a greater number of losses for which claim adjustments must
be made.

A background and knowledge of agriculture is very helpful
in landing a job as a crop adjuster and in being able to perform
the job well.

Employment opportunities also exist to be an insurance claim
adjuster for damage to vehicles, homes, and businesses. If you
specialize in vehicles, a background in body repair will be very
helpful. Knowledge of carpentry and construction will be necessary to handle losses that occur in homes and businesses.

No formal educational background or licensing is required
to become an insurance claim adjuster. One of the primary skills
insurance companies or independent adjusting companies look
for in an adjuster, though, is good human relations skills. This

is vitally important, since you will often be working with customers in a stressful situation and you must be able to convince each one that your settlement is fair. The technical and procedural aspect of adjusting is usually learned through company-sponsored, on-the-job training. Here, you may take a limited amount of classroom training and will then work with an experienced adjuster until you have developed the judgment and skill to handle claims on your own. Because this is a rather lengthy and costly training procedure, insurance companies and independent adjusting companies like to hire people who intend to stay with them for a fairly lengthy duration.

Since you are providing a service, no investment in equipment, materials, or supplies is required, other than that you have an automobile for transportation.

If you work full time seasonally, you will most likely be paid a flat amount per day, plus lodging, if necessary. If you work only on a part-time basis, you might be paid a certain rate per case handled. Regardless of the pay arrangement, insurance claim adjusters are well paid, perhaps at three to four times the minimum wage rate, since theirs is a specialized skill that cannot be performed by just anyone.

Almost any insurance company that offers agricultural, business, vehicle, or homeowner's insurance can be a good contact for you to make. Obviously, those companies that have local agents or whose policies are sold through independent insurance agencies in your community are your best prospects. Also, independent insurance adjusting companies in your area can be located through the telephone directory yellow pages.

Other moonlighting possibilities in the insurance field include selling life insurance and all sorts of homeowner's, automobile, or disability insurance through a local agency or directly for an insurance company's home office.

If you like the nature of activities performed by an insurance claim adjuster, you might also consider becoming a *real estate appraiser.*

Interior Decorator

IF YOU know which colors go with what and are knowledgeable about wall coverings, furniture styles, wall hangings, decorations, floor coverings, and everything else that belongs inside of a home or office, you have the tools to moonlight as an *interior decorator*.

As an interior decorator, your first activity is to learn all that you can about your clients so you can judge what they will find to be acceptable in the way of interior design and decorations. Information about personality, interests, tastes, goals, ambitions, self-image, background, personal preferences, and anything else that affects life-style will be particularly helpful. Then, armed with this insight and your own technical skill and knowledge, you can intelligently make recommendations to your clients concerning how their property should be decorated.

Your goal, always, should be to coordinate colors, installations, furnishings, and decorations that are in step with your clients' ideas of good taste and which are well coordinated according to professional standards.

Your activities as an interior decorator can involve developing a design for a client, securing appropriate materials, furnishings, and decorations, engaging workers to carry out the changes, and overseeing the work. You might perform all the activities described here or perhaps you will perform only some of them.

Although no particular training is required to become an interior decorator, certain skills and knowledge are necessary. Primarily, you will need to know which colors are best to reflect various moods and will need to be familiar with a wide range of building materials and decorating products. This can be learned in a number of ways, including formal study or on-the-job training. Attending seminars conducted by community colleges or manufacturers of paints, building materials, or decoration products can be very beneficial. Also, many excellent books are available on the topic and can be used for self study and for reference once you become active in the field. Interior decoration is often ideal for the person with a background or flair in design, home economics, or art.

In addition to the technical knowledge, creativity and imagination are essential attributes that a good interior decorator should possess.

You can either be a free-lance interior decorator or you can work as an employee of a decoration center or department store. In either case, your activities will be essentially the same. The primary difference is that as a free-lancer, you must develop your own clients, but you can secure your materials and furnishings from any source you wish. As an employee of a specific company, many clients will be drawn to you because of the company's reputation, products, or special sales; you will therefore need to do very little, if any, prospecting for customers. You will be limited, however, to using entirely or mostly your employer's products in your decoration projects.

If you are a free-lance interior decorator, you should develop a working relationship with contractors, paint stores, wallpaper shops, decoration centers, carpet stores, furniture dealers, and others who deal in products used in decorating. Many of them will be happy to recommend your services, since it may increase their chances of making a sale. Most of them will also give you a 15 to 20 percent discount on all products you purchase. Since you will ordinarily charge your customers regular retail price, you will make an additional profit on this override.

As an interior decorator, you are primarily providing a service. Therefore, you may have little investment in equipment and supplies. If you free-lance in this business, however, you may need to purchase or lease samples of carpet, wallpaper, drapery materials, and other goods that you can carry with you for your clients to observe. If you become involved in the actual hands-on decorating, you will also need a variety of hand tools and perhaps some power tools. You will, of course, need a vehicle for transportation to the client's home or place of business.

If you work as an employee, you might be paid a flat salary, a percentage of the price of jobs sold, or a combination of the two. If you are a free-lance interior decorator, you can charge by the hour or can set a flat amount for each job. In addition, you will earn a profit on the sale of decoration products. Since many interior decoration projects run into the thousands of dollars, you may need to do only a few jobs per year to earn the part-time income you require.

Another possibility for using your knowledge of coordination, design, and decoration is to offer your services as an *interior decoration consultant*. Here, you would simply offer advice and would not become involved in the decoration of the structure. Your clients would do that themselves or hire someone else to do it.

Lawn and Landscape Service

IF YOU like working in the great outdoors, enjoy physical work that isn't *too* physical, and want to see the immediate results of your labors, you should consider operating a *lawn and landscape service*.

In operating this business, you might mow lawns, rake leaves, trim hedges, and plant trees, bushes, and shrubs. Perhaps you will apply lawn fertilizer and weed killers and water lawns during a dry season. You might seed a lawn and nurture it to growth or sod the lawn for quick results. You can operate any of these services or all of them and more, depending upon your interests and what your customers expect of you.

One way to offer your service is as a *groundskeeper* for a

specific business like a mobile-home court, hotel, or motel. You might even contract as a *cemetery caretaker* or *church groundskeeper*. Individuals are another good class of customers. The elderly and those who are extremely busy, travel frequently, own vacation homes or who dislike this type of work are all excellent prospects.

Real estate agents are also good contacts, since they are often charged with the care and maintenance of vacant homes. Lending institutions, who on occasion foreclose on homes, should be contacted for the same reason. Property managers, apartment-building managers, and owners of real estate investment property are others who can use your services. Also, owners of condominiums or cooperative apartments contribute a monthly association fee for hiring someone to maintain the grounds, which provides another whole range of potential clients.

The amount of equipment you will need depends upon the variety of services you offer and how many clients you accept. On one end of the spectrum, only a push lawn mower and rake are needed. On the other end, a riding mower, push mower, rakes, hedge trimmer, sod cutter, other miscellaneous tools, and a van or truck to haul them will be necessary. Correspondingly, your investment may range from using only tools and equipment you already have to buying several hundred or thousand dollars' worth.

Set your fees to yield an income that is two to five times the minimum wage rate, whether you charge by the hour, the job, or the season. Exactly what you can charge will vary with the type of services you provide, type of customer, and your geographic location.

If you land more jobs than you can handle, which undoubtedly will happen if you promote your service properly, you can hire other moonlighters or students to assist you.

If your service regularly consists of applying seeds, fertilizers, weed killers, and the like, and planting trees, bushes, and shrubs, you should make an arrangement with garden centers and other suppliers whereby you receive a discount of say 15 to 20 percent on all items purchased from them. You will bill your customers at the regular retail price, thus earning a profit on each sale. If you wish, of course, you can pass all or part this savings on to your customers.

You might also consider operating a nursery, where you grow plantings for direct sale to consumers or for sale to greenhouses and garden centers. If you have a half-acre or more of fertile ground, you might operate a *sod farm*, where you grow high-quality sod for sale to contractors, homeowners, and, yes, operators of lawn and landscape services. You might also operate a *gardening service*, where you till and cultivate gardens.

Another outdoor activity that can be easily pursued on a part-time basis is that of *firewood supplier*. Here, you would cut up trees into firewood for sale to people with fireplaces or wood-burning stoves. It is easy to see how this would operate if you live in or near a rural area, but it can also be profitable if you live in a city. This can be done by cutting up trees or branches that have been felled by wind, which are marked for removal by the city Streets Department, which are cut down to clear a construction site, or which homeowners want cut down and removed. A few ads in the newspaper stating you will remove trees inexpensively (don't do it free unless there's no other way to get the trees) should bring many calls.

If you live in a northern climate, you can keep busy in the off season by operating a *snow-removal service*. This is a good way to provide year-round service to your clients and to make contacts for new customers for your lawn and landscape service or other offerings.

This entire area offers much potential for seasonal or year-round moonlighting. It can be an excellent family business and is particularly well suited for involving teen-agers who are not quite old enough, legally, for a "regular job."

Lifeguard

There's a way to keep your head above water, both financially and literally—by moonlighting as a *lifeguard*.

You have probably seen many lifeguards on duty and are therefore familiar with the activities they perform. Primarily, they supervise people's actions at a swimming pool, beach, or other swimming area. The lifeguard must focus attention on the swimmers at all times and must stand ready to spring into immediate action to rescue someone who is floundering in the water. The lifeguard must also be able to apply artificial respiration, if necessary.

Although most states do not specifically set requirements that must be met before someone can become a lifeguard, virtually anyone who hires a lifeguard has certain qualifications in mind. Paramount of these is that the applicant be certified by the American Red Cross by having passed the Advanced Lifesaving and Water Safety course. This course consists of 24 hours of instruction in lifesaving techniques and water safety. In order to take the course, you must be at least 15 years old and have passed the Basic Rescue and Water Safety course, which is 6 hours in length. If you have not taken the basic course, however, you can take it and the advanced course at the same time.

The advanced course is usually offered in 10 two-hour or 8 three-hour sessions. The registration fee is minimal, set to cover only the cost of books and film usage. The Advanced Lifesaving and Water Safety certification is granted for three years. At the end of that time, a short retraining is required before recertification is granted.

In addition to this American Red Cross certification, employers expect lifeguards to be alert and conscientious. They must exercise good judgment, possess good human relations skills, command respect, and be able to think quickly in pressure-packed emergency situations.

In order to be fully employable as a lifeguard, you should also be certified in Water Safety Instruction, also known as WSI. This allows you to teach certified American Red Cross swimming lessons at all levels, which many employers expect their lifeguards to do.

The minimum age requirement to receive WSI certification, which is granted by the American Red Cross, is 17 years old. The course consists of 30 hours of instruction, which is often presented in 15 two-hour or 10 three-hour sessions. The cost is minimal. The WSI certification must be renewed yearly, and you must teach sometime during the year in order to be eligible for renewal.

You can contact your local American Red Cross office for specific dates when Advanced Lifesaving and Water Safety and Water Safety Instruction courses are offered in your area.

Opportunities for employment as a lifeguard exist anywhere there are swimming pools, beaches, or other swimming areas. These include pools owned by municipalities, YMCAs, YWCAs, private health clubs, country clubs, individuals, colleges, public schools, and organizations of all types. Pools found at apartment complexes, condominiums, and hotels are other good possibilities. Since many of these pools are open 12 hours or so per day, 7 days per week, excellent opportunities exist for a moonlighter to work a short shift of say 4 or 5 hours, or to spell the regular lifeguards on weekends and during vacations.

The rate paid to part-time lifeguards is often not high— perhaps minimum wage or two to three times that rate at most. Being a lifeguard is not strenuous work, however, it can be an almost leisurely way to earn extra money, meet many fun-loving people, and work on your tan at the same time.

You can also moonlight as a *swimming instructor,* charging a set rate per hour or per course. If your students pay you directly, however, you will be unable to provide American Red Cross certification for your graduates, since that is not allowed. Therefore, you will need to teach those who are more interested in learning to swim than receiving certification—adults or swim-team members, for instance. You can also teach for an American Red Cross-sponsored program, which in turn will pay you.

Life Insurance Sales

Here's a little life insurance quiz. Question 1: Why does it seem that the world is overrun by life insurance sales-people? Question 2: How many average life insurance policies—with, say, a $300 annual premium—can a part-time life insurance salesperson sell in a 20-hour week? Question 3: How much income will a life insurance salesperson make from the sale of one average-size policy?

Now for the answers. Answer 1: The reason that there are seemingly so many people selling life insurance is that it is a relatively easy profession to enter and that the income potential is phenomenal, among other reasons. Answer 2: The tendency might be to overestimate the number of sales that can be made in a 20-hour week, but a goal of one or two sales would be reasonable. Answer 3: This might surprise you, and it will vary from company to company, but the salesperson will probably earn at least $315 from the sale of a single policy with a $300 annual premium. Intrigued? Well, let's explore the life insurance sales business a little further.

The first step to becoming a life insurance salesperson is to become licensed. The requirement varies from state to state, but ordinarily this amounts to passing a single exam administered by the State Insurance Commission. The test is ordinarily not difficult, but since the life insurance business has terminology and procedures all its own, it is imperative to study for the exam and to be well prepared. The information you learn in preparation for the exam is practical in that you will need to know this data to be able to perform as a life insurance salesperson anyway. Therefore, in effect, your preparation for the state exam is also a life insurance training program as well.

Usually, the State Insurance Commission offers a booklet, at a minimal cost, from which you can study for the exam. In addition, life insurance books available from commercial bookstores, college bookstores, and public and college libraries can be studied. Often, colleges and universities offer daytime or evening courses in life insurance principles that may be worth taking.

Many specialized life insurance institutes offer one-, two-, or three-day "cram" sessions on the days immediately preceding the test date. These are usually offered in the city where the test is administered. These cram sessions should not be used as a substitute for thorough study and preparation for the exam, but they may be considered to help add the final touch to your preparation. These seminars are usually expensive, say $50 to $100 per day. If you are well prepared and have done a thorough job of studying, these seminars will be unnecessary. Once you have filed your application to take the insurance exam, most likely a number of these institutes will secure your name and contact you via direct mail.

Selecting an insurance company to work for is of vital importance. There are about 1,700 life insurance companies in the country, so you have a lot to choose from. Most of the companies welcome part-time salespeople; in fact, some of the most successful agencies in the country have consisted entirely of part-timers! Factors to consider when selecting a life insurance company to sell for include the following:

Company's Reputation: Since most life insurance companies do little or no advertising, many of the biggest and best companies are relatively unknown to the average person. Therefore, don't eliminate a company just because you have never heard of it. Do select a company, however, that is well established and that has a proven record of growth.

Company's Training Program: Some life insurance companies offer a great deal of training to their salespeople; others offer little. Select one that will provide a thorough training program as well as retraining once you are actively involved in sales.

Company's General Agent: Your closest contact with the company will be through the general agent who hires you. Most likely, this person is your boss, adviser, and training director. Get to know the general agent and determine if your perspectives match before joining the organization.

Commission Rate: Part-time life insurance salespeople are paid on a commission basis, receiving a percentage of the policy premium. The commission rate and arrangement varies from company to company, so you should find a company that pays well. Usually, a part-time life insurance salesperson receives a substantial percentage of the premium paid by the policyholder in the first year, often ranging from 50 to 70 percent of the first year's premium.

The feature that makes life insurance sales a lucrative business, however, is *renewals.* That is, for a certain number of years, perhaps 9 or 10, the salesperson receives a smaller percentage of the annual premium paid by the policyholder. This might range from 5 to 10 percent of the annual premium. Thus, in calculating the total commission earned by a part-time salesperson from the sale of one $300-annual-premium policy, both the first year's earnings and the subsequent renewals must be considered. Assume that the salesperson receives a 60 percent first-year commission and 5 percent renewals for the next nine years. The first-year commission would be $180 ($300 premium × 60% = $180). The total renewals over 9 years would be $135 ($300 annual premium × 5% commission × 9 years = $135). The salesperson's total earnings would therefore be $315 ($180 first-year commission + $135 renewals = $315) from the sale of just one $300 annual-premium policy.

A variation in the first-year commission rate or in the renewal rate changes the total commission earned considerably. For example, if the salesperson received a 70 percent first-year commission rate and a 10 percent renewal rate for an additional 9 years, the total commission earned from the sale of one $300 annual-premium policy would be $480.

Sales Bonuses: Some companies include part-time salespeople in sales contests and consider them for various bonuses; others do not. Obviously, it is to your advantage to be included.

Advancement Opportunities: Numerous full-time life insurance agents started out part-time, found the business to be exciting and lucrative, and subsequently became full-time salespeople. Therefore, it is prudent to select a company that offers a good arrangement for you, should you decide to pursue the business full-time.

Of all the sales activities, prospecting for customers is one of the most important in the life insurance business. Since prospects will rarely seek you out, you must identify them, contact them, and convince them that you have a product that will fit their needs. The local newspaper is a good source of names, and you should contact the newly engaged, recently married, parents of a new child, and persons who have received a job promotion. Persons who have received building permits are also good prospects, since they will need additional mortgage insurance.

Since people buy life insurance as many as six or eight times during their lifetime (when they get married, when each child is born, when a home is purchased, when income increases, etc.), most of your customers can develop into good repeat buyers. In fact, the first three to five years in the life insurance business are the hardest; after that, your established customers will provide much of your new business.

Little investment is required to enter the life insurance sales business. Primarily, you need a serviceable automobile and suitable clothing so you look the part of a professional salesperson.

The cost of obtaining a license is generally low, in the $15 to $35 range, and annual renewal fees are similar.

Life insurance sales can be an ideal moonlighting activity for both men and women. It can match well with almost any type of regular, full-time job, since you can select the days (or nights) and hours that you want to work, by appointment, and can do much of the prospecting work from your own home via telephone.

If this type of personal sales appeals to you, *investment security sales, mutual fund sales,* and *real estate sales* should also be considered.

Locksmith

THE STRONG desire that people have for safety and the need that businesses have for security gives rise to a good moonlighting opportunity with thousands of potential customers in your immediate area—being a *locksmith.*

As a locksmith, you will install, change, and repair locks. If someone locks their keys inside their home or car, or loses their keys, you might pick the lock to gain entry or make new keys for the lock. Another major activity is to rekey locks for apartment owners, schools, businesses, and individuals. Here, you will reset the existing lock's pins and make keys to fit the new setting. Similarly, you might reset a combination lock's inner mechanisms to change the combination to open a vault or safe. Other locksmith activities include making duplicate keys for customers and devising and installing security lock and alarm systems.

You can learn to be a locksmith through on-the-job training by working for an experienced locksmith or by taking a course offered by a locksmith school or institute. Some of these schools offer correspondence programs where you complete both textbook and practical-application lessons at home. Others offer a concentrated on-campus program of perhaps 10 to 12 weeks' duration. Locksmith schools you may wish to contact for information about specific training programs include Belsaw Institute, 6301 Equitable Road, Kansas City, MO 64111; Golden Gate School of Lock Technicians, 3722 San Pablo Avenue, Emeryville, CA 94608; Locksmithing Institute, 1500 Cardinal Drive, Little Falls, NJ 07424; and New York School of Locksmithing and Alarms, 152 West 42nd Street, New York, NY 10036. Some vocational-technical schools offer a one- or two-year program that includes training in management, accounting, and other business areas as well as the technical locksmith courses.

Ordinarily, no previous training or background, including a high school diploma, is required to enter a locksmith school or to become a locksmith. A high school diploma or its equivalent is probably necessary to enter a vocational-technical school program, however.

Mechanical ability, manual dexterity, good eyesight, and the ability to work without supervision are usually necessary for success as a locksmith.

Most states do not require a license or permit in order to become a locksmith; however, many counties and cities do. The license is ordinarily easy to obtain; you will probably be finger-printed and required to pay a modest fee.

You can be a part-time employee for an established locksmith or work for a large company that needs regular locksmith services. If you are an employee, all materials, equipment, and supplies will most likely be furnished for you, so your investment will be nil. You will probably be paid an hourly rate, which might be two to four times the minimum wage rate.

Another possibility that holds good income and growth potential is to operate your own locksmith business. In this case, you will need to secure a variety of tools and equipment, including files, screwdrivers, calipers, vices, hacksaws, hammers, chisels, and specialized locksmith gear. Blank keys and lock-cleaning materials and supplies will also be required. If you specialize in small jobs, your total investment might be only a few hundred dollars. If you conduct a complete, full-range locksmith and security-device operation, your investment may well reach several thousand dollars.

Locksmith tools, materials, and supplies can be purchased from a locksmith supplier. You may wish to contact the National Locksmith Suppliers Association, 99 West Hawthorne Avenue, Valley Stream, NY 11580, for information.

You can operate your part-time locksmithing business out of your home or from a commercial location, or you might equip a van or other vehicle as a portable locksmith shop.

A locksmith's charges are ordinarily based on an hourly rate, which is often three to five times the minimum wage rate. In addition, profit is made from the sale of locks and other products.

Being a locksmith can be interesting and self-satisfying work. On occasion, you will get emergency calls that need immediate attention, but most jobs can be arranged to easily fit in with your normal schedule.

For more information about locksmiths, contact the national locksmiths organization: Associated Locksmiths of America, 3003 Live Oak Street, Dallas, TX 75204.

If this general line of work appeals to you, but locks do not, you might consider becoming a *gunsmith* or operating a *watch repair service*. Entry procedures, work activities, and income potential are similar to that of a locksmith.

Manufacturer's Employee

For those who prefer "just plain working" to jobs that require formal education, managerial talent, paper shuffling, and risk taking, the ideal moonlighting activity may be as a *manufacturer's employee*. It's not that skill isn't necessary to be a manufacturer's employee—plenty of that is often required—but it's a *different* type of skill.

As a manufacturer's employee you will work on an assembly line, or in maintenance, cleanup, shipping, delivery, or some other activity. Some of these jobs require training and/or experience, while others may require nothing but a willingness to work and an average amount of common sense.

Opportunities exist with large manufacturers, yes, but it is often smaller companies not bound by rigid union contracts that offer the best employment possibilities. Any size manufacturer is worth checking, however. Manufacturing companies located in college communities are particularly good prospects since many of them regularly schedule short work shifts to accommodate student class schedules. They do not, however, limit their part-time work force to students.

An advantage of being a manufacturer's employee is that you ordinarily have no investment in supplies, equipment, materials, or anything else. You show up for work, do your job, and get paid. It is simple and direct without worries and concerns. Often, the pay rate is high, two to six times the minimum wage rate, and the work is steady. This, coupled with the other advantages, makes working as a manufacturer's employee an attractive way to moonlight.

Opportunities also exist to do *home assembly* for some manufacturers. This means that you pick up the raw materials or components from the company, take them home for processing or assembly, and return the finished product on your next daily or weekly visit. This arrangement is not possible with many manufacturers, but it is often ideal for those who manufacture a small product that is easily hand assembled or for which little training is required. Manufacturers of handmade jewelry, novelty items, handcrafted leather items, and hand-tied fishing lures are among those worth contacting.

Payment is usually on the piecework basis, meaning you get paid at a set rate per item produced. The rate of pay can be very satisfactory if you are a good self-starter and can work industriously without supervision.

The small one- or two-person *home-based manufacturer* is still another possibility to consider. Those making ornamental iron works, hand-built furniture, Christmas decorations, picnic tables, leather goods, business signs, or dozens of other products may delight in having a hardworking part-time helper. An advantage of working at this level of manufacturing can be that you get the opportunity to work on all phases of the product and can get involved in design, product development, and distribution. Also, if the idea ever really catches on (as has happened many times), you are in on the ground floor, and a fantastic future may await you. The disadvantage is that since the operation is so small, its income may likewise be small. Therefore, your pay may be low or undependable.

If you like the manufacturing area, have ideas of your own, and possess ingenuity, drive, and ambition, you might consider starting your own *independent manufacturing company.* Sound like a big job? Well, it can be, but you will not, of course, attempt to become General Motors overnight.

Develop an idea for a product that fills a need and that you have the ability to make; then get started. Perhaps you can begin in your home, basement, garage, or outbuilding with little investment required for facilities or equipment, other than what you already have. Proceed slowly, step by step, and resist the temptation of trying to get too big too fast. If necessary, seek the professional advice of a patent attorney to determine if your product should be patented.

Since this is a secondary activity, in addition to your regular job, you may be able to plough all profits back into the business until it really gets rolling or at least until it is on a solid basis. After that, you can draw out most of the profits and you will have established your moonlighting income by your own efforts.

Modeling

Perhaps the mere mention of the term *model* conjures up thoughts of a strikingly beautiful woman or suavely handsome man posing for a photographic session for a high-fashion magazine or advertising agency. This is an accurate image, especially in the competitive New York modeling world, but there are numerous other opportunities available, for the person who is interested in *modeling*.

Business and industry provide many opportunities for the model. These include displaying and promoting products like furniture, automobiles, audio equipment, and just about anything imaginable at trade shows and conventions. The model serves as a host or hostess, attracting the attention of prospective customers, and might even take an active role in demonstrating and explaining the product. A similar role is often portrayed by models at grand openings, at open houses, and for new-product announcements at retail stores and manufacturers' showrooms. Sometimes, models are employed to give tours of the company's facilities or to greet and assist company personnel, stockholders, and guests at sales meetings, the annual stockholder's meeting, and other company-sponsored activities.

Many retail clothing stores use models to promote the sale of their wares. The store might conduct a fashion show, or models might walk through the store, stopping to pose for customers and to describe the garments they are wearing. Often, models are called upon to provide a similar service at the store's restaurant or at a nearby restaurant in the same shopping center or emporium. During the lunch hour, the model moves from table to table, posing and describing the outfit and accessories.

Fashion shows are another area of opportunity. Some of these are presented by clothing designers or manufacturers for retail store owners and merchandise buyers in an attempt to sway them to stock their lines. Other fashion shows are conducted by retail stores to encourage their customers, the consumers, to buy.

Advertising agencies are another major user of models' services. Photographs are taken of all sorts of consumer products including cosmetics, cleansers, detergents, nonprescription drugs, tools, office equipment, industrial equipment, and almost anything else. The photographs are used in magazine and newspaper advertisements and in company brochures, pamphlets, posters, and catalogs.

Other opportunities exist for artist's models and for those who specialize in television commercials.

The top models have outstanding looks. This does not necessarily mean that every model must be a beautiful woman or handsome man. For some products and types of modeling, an outstanding appearance is necessary, yes. For others, however, like advertisements for floor wax, detergents, and bulldozers, enviable good looks are out of place; a more ordinary-looking person is appropriate—an ordinary-looking person with character, to be exact.

Though the age range for high-fashion models usually starts in the mid-teens and ends in the early thirties, many opportunities exist for modeling of one type or another for persons of almost any age.

Qualities required to become a model depend on the type of modeling you do. In general, poise, carriage, bearing, posture, confidence, and grooming must be well developed. A knowledge of makeup, clothes selection and coordination, and hairstyles is also necessary. In some modeling roles, polished speaking skills are also often required.

One way to learn to be a model is to attend a modeling school. A short course offered on weekends or evenings will be helpful. Once you have learned the basic idea of what you should do, you can practice on your own to develop your skills. Training in the theater, or even experience in high school, college, or community plays, will be helpful as well.

Businesses, advertising agencies, and others who frequently use models usually rely on modeling agencies to provide their personnel. Therefore, one of your first steps toward landing a job as a part-time model is to register with a modeling agency. If the agency feels you have potential, it will attempt to find suitable work for you. Modeling agencies can be located through the yellow pages of most city telephone directories. If there are no specialized modeling agencies in your area, contact entertainment booking agencies, who most likely book models as well as other clients.

Since some models are employed by a specific retail store, business, or convention center, you might even make your own direct contacts, just as you would if applying for any other type of job.

In some cases, models furnish their own clothing for the job, while in other situations it is provided for them. Other than that, a model's costs are usually limited to the purchase of various cosmetics and grooming products and services.

Pay arrangements for models vary with the type of modeling activity. Photographic models are usually paid by the hour, while those working trade shows and conventions may be paid by the day or receive a flat amount for the event. Retail store models are paid by the hour or on a weekly or monthly salary. Earnings can vary considerably, with a retail store model receiving anywhere from perhaps two to ten times the minimum wage rate and a high-fashion model receiving several hundred dollars per hour. The possibility always exists that you will come to the attention of an advertising company executive or photographer who is looking for that "special look" you possess, and you could be on your way to fame and fortune! That may not be a likely occurrence, but it is a pleasant thought to keep in the back of one's mind.

The greatest modeling opportunities exist in the large cities. Because of the wide range of uses for a model's talents, however, good potential also exists in the outlying areas, and the competition for jobs may not be as tough.

Modeling often provides sporadic employment, even for those who are full-time models. Therefore, it can be an ideal moonlighting activity. Since much of the business and industry modeling is done on evenings or weekends, that time schedule might easily fit into your regular routine.

A knowledge of modeling can lead to other exciting and satisfying part-time jobs. One possibility is to serve as a *consultant* to those sponsoring fashion shows and to area beauty pageants. You might also conduct *grooming and charm seminars* for groups and associations or teach modeling as an evening or weekend course for a community college or modeling school in your area.

You could even establish your own *modeling school,* which operates on a full-time, evening, or weekend basis. The business world also holds several possibilities such as being a *fashion consultant* or *merchandise buyer* for a retail clothier. If you like the business end of modeling, you might even establish your own *model booking agency.* In fact, many opportunities exist in a wide range of employment areas for a person with poise, carriage, confidence, and a knowledge of how to present his or her best image.

Music on Wheels

How's your music I.Q.? Well, if you know the type of music that is popular today and can recognize songs that have a good dance beat, you are well equipped to moonlight with *music on wheels.* Music on wheels? Perhaps a short explanation is in order.

As the cost of live musical entertainment has soared, many schools, colleges, private clubs, organizations, and even nightclubs have found that they cannot afford this luxury. What do they do for musical entertainment then? The next best solution is often to turn to nationally known entertainers—in the form of recorded music. The problem, however, is that many of these users have a need for musical entertainment only occasionally. Therefore, they cannot afford the expense of buying a high-powered sound system and a wide collection of records for one or two nights of use. This is where music on wheels comes in.

Music on wheels is a traveling musical entertainment show. You need only three basic pieces of equipment and you're ready to go. First, you need a high-quality sound system with enough power to provide clear, clean, music in a variety of locations including dance halls, gymnasiums, nightclubs, or any other place where dances might be held. Second, you need a wide selection of popular records. Third, a vehicle or two-wheel trailer is necessary to transport your equipment.

Ideally, the sound equipment should be installed in a portable cabinet that can be easily wheeled or carried. Speakers can be built in, and auxiliary speakers might be used as well. This portable feature is necessary since the service you provide will ordinarily consist of a series of one-night stands, and you will need to set up and tear down quickly and easily.

A public address (PA) system should be built into your portable unit so you can announce songs and talk to the audience.

Your records should be cataloged for easy reference and they should be housed in easily transportable cases.

An additional flair can be added by developing a portable light show with colors and flashing lights to create various moods.

The high-quality equipment needed to provide music on wheels is expensive, and a substantial investment will be needed to establish a suitable collection of records. Often, however, excellent used equipment can be purchased from professional musicians or from nightclub operators who no longer operate a disco. The cost of this used equipment will be a fraction of what it would cost new. The portable cabinet to house the equipment will most likely need to be custom made. This can be built with sturdy plywood and other commonly available building materials.

Since you will be buying a large number of records, you can probably work out a discount arrangement with a retailer who will be anxious to have your account.

Promote your business by mailing professionally printed flyers to all area junior high schools, high schools, colleges, nightclubs, and any organizations that might need entertainment. Also place advertisements in newspapers and other publications to attract individuals who will sponsor private parties or wedding dances.

In advance of each appearance, provide your customer with large, attractive, professionally printed posters that can be displayed to announce the event. This helps the sponsor make it a success—and it is excellent free advertising for you as well.

Keep in mind that your job is to *entertain* your audience. This means that you must be responsive to their moods and tastes when you select music to play. Since each audience may have its own character, your show may vary considerably from one night to the next.

Since most dances and parties where musical entertainment is provided are at night, music on wheels can be an ideal moonlighting activity. Because your unit is portable, you can offer your service in a wide geographic area, perhaps a radius of 50 to 100 miles from your home base. Weekends will provide the biggest demand for your service, but other possibilities, especially at colleges and nightclubs, exist for weeknights as well. If your service is well promoted, you can probably perform two to four times per week.

Your fee should be significantly lower than what live musical entertainment would cost your customers. The amount you can charge will vary with your local situation, but you should be able to earn a minimum of $100 per night and may well command up to three times that amount. With this income potential, you can quickly recoup your initial investment in equipment.

Music on wheels can be an ideal moonlighting activity for the music lover. In addition to earning outstanding money, it is a great way to build your own record collection and obtain a first-class sound system. And helping people have a good time might be the best reward of all.

National Guard

HERE'S A moonlighting opportunity that offers camaraderie, challenge, and a chance to get experience—and it's patriotic! You can join the *National Guard*.

Actually, the term *National Guard* isn't as accurate to use as *National Guards,* since there are two of them—the Army National Guard and the Air Force National Guard. The information in this article pertains to the Army National Guard, but the procedures and opportunities in both units are similar.

In order to join the National Guard, a person with no prior military experience needs to be a high school graduate or hold an equivalency certificate, must be between ages 17 and 34, and must be mentally, physically, and morally fit. An eight-week basic training session is served at a military base, followed by specialized training of 5 to 16 weeks, depending upon the area of specialization.

A person with prior military experience can join the National Guard without going through basic training and usually without any additional specialized training. A person with 20 years or more of military service can usually join up until they are age 50 or 60, depending on their state's regulation. Those with less than 20 years' experience who are beyond age 34 can still join if they will be able to complete their 20 years before they reach the 50- or 60-year age limit.

All Guard members serve one weekend per month with their local unit and participate in an annual two-week training session at a training site. In addition, the Guard unit might be activated upon the governor's orders to assist in security and to help with cleanup of damage caused by a flood, tornado, or other natural disaster. Also, the Guard might be activated to help quell a prison riot or similar disturbance. In case of a national emergency, the Guard unit can be called to active military duty.

By law, employers are required to allow employees to participate in National Guard activities, including basic training and ensuing specialized training, with a right for the employee to reenter the job upon return. The employer is not required to pay wages for this time away from the job. Even though the employee participates in the annual two-week training session and may also miss work because the Guard was activated for some state emergency, the employee is still entitled to normal vacation time.

Persons with no prior military experience must enlist in the National Guard for an initial six-year period. This can be served as six years of active Guard duty, or as three years of active duty and three years in the inactive reserve pool. Those with prior military experience can enlist for a minimum of one to three years, depending upon rank and experience.

Guard members who move to a new community can transfer to the unit in that area. If justifiable circumstances merit it,

Guard members can usually receive an honorable discharge before their enlistment period expires. A person who simply quits will probably receive a less-than-honorable discharge.

The rank at which a person with no prior military experience enters the National Guard depends upon educational background. A person with a high school diploma or its equivalent enters as a Pvt. 1; a person with two years of college enters as a Pvt. 2; and a graduate of a four-year college enters as a Pvt. 3 (Private First Class, or PFC).

The rank determines the amount of pay received during basic, specialized, and annual training and for weekend sessions. Currently, a Pvt. 1 receives $551 per month for the basic, specialized, and annual two-week training sessions and receives $73 per weekend session. A Pvt. 2 receives $618 and $82, and a PFC receives $642 and $90 for the same periods. A Guard member with dependents receives an additional $205 per month for basic, specialized, and annual training periods, but weekend pay is not affected. Persons with prior military experience and a higher rank than illustrated here will receive a higher pay rate when they join the Guard. Guard members also receive their military clothing and food while in training status.

Each Guard member receives an annual rate increase, because of increased experience, and the basic rate schedule is adjusted every two years. Guard members can also receive a pay increase by being promoted to a higher rank. A Pvt. 1 with six months' Guard experience can probably be promoted to Pvt. 2. Promotion from Pvt. 2 to PFC can probably be attained in about four months. Promotions beyond that are also attainable.

The National Guard often offers a bonus program to encourage enlistments. Whether or not a bonus is granted and the amount of bonus are determined by each unit's needs and the area of specialization entered. Cash bonuses of $1,500 to $2,000 or a $1,000-per-year college allowance for four years are possible.

Those who have completed the initial National Guard enlistment period may reenlist for minimum periods of one to three years, depending upon their amount of military experience. Reenlistment bonuses are sometimes offered.

A person with 20 years of National Guard experience or of combined military and Guard experience is eligible for a retirement program. Retirement benefits start at age 60.

Specific National Guard requirements and procedures vary slightly from state to state. Therefore, you should contact your area National Guard headquarters for more information.

Other possibilities to earn part-time income while serving your country exist with reserve units of the Air Force, Army, Navy, Marines, and Coast Guard. Entrance requirements, activities, pay, and other features are similar to the National Guard, although they are exempted from being activated for state emergencies.

Pawnbroker

ARE YOU shrewd? Do you fit the image of a wheelerdealer? If so, you may have the perfect disposition to moonlight as a *pawnbroker*.

Perhaps you have a general idea of what a pawnbroker does, but let's look at some specifics. Primarily, people who are in need of cash fast come to the pawnbroker for a short-term loan. As security for the loan, they pledge, or pawn, some article of personal property like jewelry, appliances, or sporting equipment. The borrower and the pawnbroker sign an agreement that the borrower is to repay the loan, plus interest, by some specific date and reclaim the property. If the loan is not repaid, ownership of the pawned property transfers to the pawnbroker, who can then sell it and retain the entire sales price. In some cases, the owner-borrower has no intention of reclaiming the property, so the pawnbroker buys the article outright.

To be a successful pawnbroker, you must know the value of property so that you do not loan more than the item is worth. Ordinarily, pawnbrokers loan far less than an article's current value. For example, if a borrower had purchased a new portable typewriter for $300 a year ago and it would be readily salable today in used condition for $100, the pawnbroker might lend $50 to $60 on it. Therefore, if the borrower fails to repay the loan and reclaim the typewriter, the pawnbroker stands to make a substantial profit when he or she eventually sells it, presumably at $100.

The best way to develop a feel for determining an article's current value is through experience. A large collection of consumer product catalogs will serve as good reference material, and a knowledge of what used products sell for at secondhand stores and auctions will be helpful.

Pawnbrokers assume a high degree of risk, based on the fact that items not reclaimed may not sell for many months and that their eventual sales price is unknown. Therefore, pawnbrokers charge a high rate of interest. An annual percentage rate of 25 to 40 percent, or even more, is not uncommon. The rate that can be charged is regulated by usury laws in some states or cities but not in others.

Licensing required to become a pawnbroker varies widely from state to state and even from city to city within a state. In some states and cities, there are no specific regulations. Check with your State Department of Banking or State Department of Financial Institutions and with your city clerk to see what regulations exist and to determine maximum interest rates that can be charged. Ordinarily, the regulations are not very restrictive and it is easy to become a pawnbroker. In those areas where licenses are required, they are usually renewable on an annual basis.

If a pawnbroker deals in firearms, a *federal pawnbroker's license* must be acquired from the Bureau of Alcohol, Tobacco, and Firearms. To obtain this license, you must complete an application, your background will be checked, and an inspector will contact you. There are specific requirements to be met, but, basically, if you have a clean record with no "skeletons" in your closet, you will receive the permit. The license is renewable annually by payment of a modest fee. Specific information on license requirements can be obtained from one of seven regional offices, or by contacting the Bureau of Alcohol, Tobacco, and Firearms, 1111 Constitution Avenue, N.W., Washington, DC 20226.

As a dealer in firearms, you will be required to maintain an acquisition and disposition book, called the *bound book*. Each gun that is acquired and disposed of must be recorded in it. When a firearm is reclaimed by the owner or sold, a *firearm transaction record* must be completed by the buyer. You are to keep this record in your files.

Some states also have requirements pertaining to the sale of firearms. A common regulation is that a buyer of handguns must present a state permit to the seller before the gun can be purchased. Often, the buyer obtains this permit from the county sheriff.

A pawnbroker may accept or reject any articles pledged as security for a loan that they wish. If an article is in poor condition or unsalable, or if the pawnbroker is not knowledgeable enough to determine value (as with diamond rings and guns), the pawnbroker could refuse to make the loan or to buy the item outright.

A pawnbroker must be particularly careful not to receive stolen goods as pledge for a loan or as an outright purchase. If the situation looks suspicious, you might require that proof of ownership be provided or you might check with the police or sheriff's departments to see if the article has been reported stolen. Many states or cities have a requirement that a pawnbroker must keep each article a certain time period, perhaps 30 days, before it is offered for resale. This gives law enforcement authorities time to check your inventory to search for stolen goods. If you do possess a stolen article, it will be taken from you, returned to the rightful owner, and you will lose your investment. If stolen property is found on your premises more often than is reasonable to expect of a pawnbroker, you may even lose your license or face criminal charges. If you proceed in a careful, businesslike manner, however, these severe eventualities should pose no threat to you whatsoever.

A pawnshop can be operated from a business location or from your home, unless state or city regulations prohibit the latter. You can easily operate on a part-time schedule, perhaps being open one or more days or several evenings per week.

In reality, a pawnshop is part loan office and part retail store. Therefore, you will need sufficient cash on hand to make loans and will need to set up display cases and shelves. Since the loans are short term, the cash is turned over rapidly, and you may be able to start with a surprisingly small amount of cash. Because of the nature of the business, a prime location and fancy furnishings are not necessary. Secondhand or homemade cases and shelves will be satisfactory.

Operating as a pawnbroker can be an exciting and profitable way to moonlight. You will meet many interesting people and will be able to obtain many fine consumer products for your own use at bargain prices.

If you like the idea of dealing in used merchandise but don't like the loan aspect of being a pawnbroker, you might consider establishing a *secondhand store* or *consignment and resale shop*. With a secondhand store, you will buy and sell used items. With a consignment and resale shop, you will take goods on consignment, sell them, and pay the owner a percentage of the sales price while keeping the remainder as your fee for providing the marketplace. Usually, the shop operator keeps 40 to 50 percent of the price at which goods are sold, and the owner receives the rest.

Pest Control

IF YOU don't scream at the sight of spiders or climb up on a chair when you see a mouse, you may have the proper temperament to moonlight in the field of *pest control.*

As a pest-control technician, or *exterminator,* you would rid houses, business establishments, and other structures of various pests, including cockroaches, termites, rodents, ants, fleas, silverfish, carpet beetles, clothes moths, houseflies, spiders, wasps, bees, hornets, birds, and others.

Your activities would include removing the pests from the premises through the use of pesticides, traps, bait, fumigants and other methods. A big part of the job includes location of the source of the problem and remedying it so that the infestation does not recur. This often requires a good working knowledge of the biology and habits of the pests and a keen sense of observation. Frequently, the remedy includes applying caulking or cement to cracks in walls or foundations, installing screening, or recommending structural changes.

In addition to removing pests that are already on the premises, your activities might include preventive maintenance, where you regularly service restaurants, businesses, or homes to head off any pest-control problems before they begin. Also, before Federal Housing Administration (FHA)-insured and Veteran's Administration (VA)-guaranteed loans can be granted, a termite inspection report must be filed, thus providing another good source of business.

In addition to being knowledgeable about pests and their habits, a pest-control technician must be able to evaluate the problem at hand, determine the best technique to use, and select the proper chemical, bait, trap, or other medium to solve the problem. This requires a good degree of common sense and adaptability to each new situation that arises in the field. The technician must be extremely safety conscious, with the client's health and personal welfare always being uppermost in mind. In addition, physical agility is important, since it is often necessary to inspect attics, crawl spaces, and other tight areas.

Moonlighting as a pest-control technician can be ideal for someone who already has training or knowledge in chemistry, biology, sanitation, public health services, or entomology.

Essentially, there are two employment levels in the pest-control business: the *certified applicator* and the *employee*. Each state has its own regulations, which are usually administered through the Department of Agriculture. In general, a person must have one to three years' experience (usually two) in the pest-control field and must pass a written test to become a certified applicator. In some states, all or part of the experience requirement may be waived if the applicant has experience or a solid background in a related field. Most states require that each pest-control office have a certified applicator on staff and that this person be available to supervise the activities of all other pest-control employees. An *employee* is one who works for a pest-control company as a technician, exterminating pests and performing other pest-control activities.

One way to moonlight in the pest-control field is to work as an employee for a pest-control firm, as described above. This requires no certification. Some of the large, well-known pest-control companies do not hire part-time employees, however. This is not because they necessarily have anything against part-timers but because their investment of time and money in an employee training program is not justified unless the employee works full time. Therefore, your best part-time employment opportunities may exist with local, independent companies.

A second possibility for entering the pest-control field is to establish your own company, hiring a certified applicator to meet that requirement of state law. Before proceeding with this, however, check with your state's regulatory agency to make certain this maneuver is acceptable.

A third way to enter this field is to work as an employee until you have gained the required experience to become a certified applicator yourself. Then, you can offer your own service without needing to hire a highly paid, on-staff certified applicator.

Pest-control techniques can be learned in a number of ways, including on-the-job training through working with an experienced technician or by taking university extension courses. Also, chemical and equipment manufacturers often sponsor seminars, of perhaps one to three days' duration, that can be very helpful. Then too, excellent training and reference materials can be purchased from the National Pest Control Association, 8100 Oak Street, P.O. Box 377, Dunn Loring, VA 22027.

If you work as an employee for a pest-control company, you will most likely have no investment in equipment or supplies. If you establish your own company, you will need to buy one or more pressure sprayers, dusters (to dust or "puff" pesticides into inaccessible areas), and flashlights. Various pieces of safety equipment will be necessary, and you will need a vehicle. Of course, a good stock of pesticides, traps, and other supplies will be needed. The cost of getting established can vary from several hundred dollars to thousands, depending upon the variety of pest-control services you offer.

As an employee of a pest-control company, you will most likely be paid by the hour or by the job. In either case, your earnings should be two to four times the minimum wage rate, depending upon your experience, expertise, and geographic location.

If you operate your own business, you can charge by the hour, set a flat rate for each type of job, or set your fee based upon the nature of the job and its difficulty. Whatever the method, your earnings can be high for the amount of time invested.

If you develop an interest in entering the pest-control business full time, you may wish to become affiliated with one of the large, well-known pest-control companies. Several who may be worth contacting at that point are Orkin, 2170 Piedmont Road,

N.E., Atlanta, GA 30301; Terminix International, Inc., P.O. 17167, Memphis, TN 38117; or Western Exterminator Company, 1732 Kaiser Avenue, Irvine, CA 92714.

Photographer

THE BUSINESS of capturing memories is an exciting one that can be easily pursued on a part-time basis. Capturing memories? Yes, on film, by a *photographer*.

As a photographer, you can pick an area of specialization, or you can "shoot" just about anybody or anything. Individual and group portraits are one good possibility. Others include graduation pictures, weddings, passport photographs, class reunions, and baby pictures in your studio or at retail business or shopping center promotions. If you live in a lively entertainment area, promotional pictures of musicians, actors, actresses, magicians, and others will keep you busy.

People will even pay to have professional photographs taken of their pets or treasured art objects. Real estate agents, needing high-quality photographs of homes they have listed for sale, are another source of business. Then too, there is the possibility of taking photographs of local sporting activities, social events, and items of community interest for your local newspaper.

Basic equipment you will need includes one or more professional cameras, lighting devices, and several different backdrops. A studio will be necessary if you specialize in portraits, graduation pictures, baby pictures, and other kinds of photographs where your customers come to you. This can be a room in your home, or you can rent a business location, depending upon the circumstances and the volume of work that you do. For many types of photography, the great outdoors will serve as your studio or you will go to your customer's place of business, church, or school. Be prepared to take photographs both in black and white and in color.

Advertising and promoting your service is an important aspect of being a photographer. Develop a printed price list showing the various sizes of photographs and package arrangements that you offer and distribute the list to everyone with whom you come in contact. You can also develop a form letter and send it along with a price list to the newly engaged, whose names appear in your local newspaper. Be alert to others whom you can contact in a similar manner. Timely newspaper advertisements should likewise result in your obtaining new customers. One of the best advertisements will be your photographs themselves. As people witness the quality of your work, they will be impressed and will seek you out.

You can increase your enjoyment of photography and enhance your professional prestige as well by submitting some of your better works to contests or to magazines for possible publication. Success in one of these areas will serve as excellent advertising and will allow you to obtain more customers and higher prices.

Since the income potential from each photo session is high, often several hundred dollars, your earnings as a part-time photographer can be excellent. Even though some customers might expect your rates to be lower than a full-time photography studio's, it is your quality that they are buying, and you should be able to charge competitive prices.

Virtually all your photo sessions will be by appointment, allowing you flexibility in coordinating this moonlighting activity with your other responsibilities.

You can increase your profit by operating a *film development laboratory*, where you process your own black-and-white film. You might even expand that service to development of color film for your own use and for customers like drugstores and camera shops.

Another good possibility for increasing income from photography is to operate a *framing studio,* where you build picture frames for sale to your customers and others.

Piano Tuner

Cᴀɴ ʏᴏᴜ play piano—even just a little bit? If so, and if you have a "good ear," there is a moonlighting opportunity that is in perfect harmony with your abilities: you can become a *piano tuner.*

The primary activity of a piano tuner is to adjust a piano's strings so they are in tune, as the term implies. The piano tuner strikes a tuning fork or uses an electronic tuning device to identify the pitch of the middle A. Then, the piano tuner tightens or loosens the string's tuning pin, using a piano tuner's handle, until the vibration of the string matches that of the tuning fork or electronic tuning device. Next, all the other strings are tuned to intervals that produce a perfect harmony. This does not require perfect pitch, but it does require a very good ear. This is because many notes are produced by three strings and others by two strings, which are struck by a single piano hammer and therefore must vibrate at the same pitch to produce one note.

The amount of time required to tune an upright piano, as found in most homes, will vary with the piano's condition. If it is just slightly out of tune, the job can most likely be completed in less than an hour. If it is grossly out of tune, it may take three or four hours or more. The time required to tune a concert piano may be considerably greater.

Piano tuners also make minor repairs to pianos, such as replacing piano strings, keys, or felt on the piano hammers; cleaning the strings so they vibrate more freely; and regulating the piano's key action. Perhaps the most demanding activity performed by piano tuners is that of "voicing." Here, the piano's tone and quality are regulated by adjusting the key action and by tempering the level of hardness of each piano hammer's felt surface.

Basic equipment needed by a piano tuner includes a tuning fork or electronic tuning device (or perfect pitch), piano tuner's handle, rubber or felt mutes to place between strings to block out vibrations, and miscellaneous parts and supplies. The cost of getting established is relatively low, a few hundred dollars at most.

Piano tuning can be learned by working with a skilled piano tuner as an apprentice, for say a year and a half or two, or by attending a piano tuner's school for perhaps a year or so. Piano-tuning courses are even offered via mail order, although many will find this to be an extremely difficult way to learn piano tuning. Schools and colleges that offer piano-tuning curriculums include Grayson County College, 6101 Grayson Drive, Denison, TX 75020; Central Piedmont College, 1841 Kenwood Avenue, Piedmont, NC 28205; Napa College, 102 Belvedere Court, Napa, CA 94559; Perkins School of Piano Tuning and Technology, 227 Court Street, Elyria, OH 44035; Western Iowa Tech, 4647 Stone Avenue—Box 265, Sioux City, IA 51102; North Bennet Street School, 39 North Bennet Street, Boston, MA 02113; and, Douglas College, P.O. 2503, New Westminster, British Columbia, Canada VEL5B2.

Much opportunity exists for a piano tuner, and you can probably be kept as busy as you want to be. Homeowners, schools, churches, nightclubs, and even music stores will be able to regularly use your services, with some pianos needing to be tuned at least three or four times per year.

Some piano tuners charge by the hour, while others charge a flat rate regardless of the amount of time involved. Some even charge by pitch. This means that they charge a flat amount plus an extra fee for each one-fourth or one-half tone the piano is out of pitch, since the further it is off key, the longer it takes to be tuned. Regardless of the payment method, a piano tuner might easily earn four to seven times the minimum wage per hour.

An experienced and highly skilled piano tuner, who might more appropriately be called a *piano technician*, will find concert halls, professional musicians, symphonies, and renowned pianists to be exciting and profitable clients. Additional training and much experience is usually required to reach this level of the profession.

For more information on piano tuning, contact the Piano Technicians Guild, 113 Dexter Avenue North, Seattle, WA 98109.

If you have a musical background, another moonlighting activity you can consider is to operate an *instrument repair service*. School band members, school music departments, professional musicians, and others will most likely keep you very busy. You might also offer a *piano moving service*, where you relieve people of the burden of moving the heaviest and most cumbersome of all personal possessions.

Private Investigator

As A child, did you ever dream of becoming a sleuth like Sherlock Holmes? Well, now you can act out those fantasies in real life, by becoming a *private investigator*.

In truth, the cases handled by modern-day private investigators seldom are as exciting and intriguing as those encountered by Sherlock Holmes and other fictionalized characters. The job can be interesting, and it is rewarding, but there is no steady diet of hidden clues, interwoven and mysterious personalities, or suspicious-looking butlers.

Primarily, a private investigator's job is that of fact finding. This involves interviewing people, searching public records in the courthouse or city hall, and making personal inspections of accident sites. Other activities include conducting surveillance, snapping photographs, and taking other steps to gather useful information.

You might be engaged by a defense attorney in a criminal case to substantiate the alibi of the defendant, locate a witness who has disappeared, search for clues at the scene of the crime, or gather routine background information. An insurance company might have you conduct daily surveillance of a person who has filed an enormous lawsuit for "injuries" suffered at the hands of one of the insurance company's policyholders. In an attempt to prove fraud, you would stalk the person, spying on him through a peephole in a van or from long range with binoculars (just like in the movies!). Your goal would be to secure a photograph of the person in a "not-so-injured" pose.

An individual might hire you to monitor the actions of a spouse, who is suspected of various indiscretions. Likewise, a prospective bride's father might engage you to make a discreet background check on the "suspicious-looking" prospective son-in-law. Businesses might make similar use of your services to secure a background profile of a prospective employee before the person is hired for a "top secret" or important position within the company.

If you have special knowledge in the area, you might investigate the origin of fires and explosions on behalf of insurance companies, natural gas supply companies, and the like.

You might also locate missing persons for concerned family members, for a creditor trying to collect an overdue debt, or for an administrator of a will who is seeking a long-lost heir.

No specific training is ordinarily required to become a private investigator. A familiarity with law enforcement procedures, a thorough knowledge of what is contained in public records and how to find it, and a well-developed interviewing technique are among the skills that are necessary. You must also know and follow your state's statutes that apply to private investigators and must adhere to all the various privacy laws. In addition, you must be thorough, fastidious, and reliable so that you overlook nothing and file a complete and accurate report.

Licensing laws for becoming a private investigator vary widely, from no requirements, licensing, or registration at all in some states to rather strict regulations in others. In those states where licensing is required, you may need experience with a private investigation firm, police department, or sheriff's department before you can open your own firm. In some states, you must pass a written examination; other states require you to provide a mug shot, be fingerprinted, and become bonded. Check with your State Department of Public Safety to determine what regulations apply in your state.

You can either work for an existing private investigation firm or establish your own operation. If you work for someone else, you might specialize in one or two areas of investigation or handle only certain types of cases. You will be paid at an hourly rate, which is perhaps two to five times the minimum wage rate, or on a per-case basis. In those states with strict licensing regulations for private investigators, it is usually far easier to become certified to work for someone else than to set up your own firm.

An advantage of establishing your own private investigation agency is that you can accept only those cases that sound interesting, lucrative, and within your ability level and time availability. You can reject any cases or clients that you wish.

Various billing arrangements might be used to charge for your services. An hourly rate of five to ten times the minimum wage rate for actual investigation time plus a lower rate for driving time might be normal.

You might also collect a *retainer* from several of your biggest and most frequent customers. This means that they pay you an annual fee of say $1,000, $5,000, or whatever in return for your promise to be available to them a certain number of hours per week or month if they need you. Your client will pay your regular fee for any time actually worked. Obviously, you will only be able to collect a retainer from clients who view your services as being so valuable that they cannot bear facing the possibility of your being unavailable when they need you.

Relatively little investment in equipment and supplies is necessary to establish your own private investigation agency, since you are primarily providing a service. You will need a reliable automobile, a good-quality camera, a dependable battery-operated tape recorder for taping interviews, and a variety of notebooks and other inexpensive items. You will also need a telephone for business purposes. You can operate from a business location or use a portion of your home for office space.

If you develop more clients than you can personally handle, you can easily expand your operation by hiring one or more persons to help with your investigations. Expanding your staff will allow excellent opportunities for you and each of the others to specialize in some phase of investigation activity.

Another moonlighting possibility, which is somewhat similar to being a private investigator but is much simpler and easier to do, is to free-lance as an *investigative photographer*. Here, you will go about your daily or nightly activities around your home while you constantly monitor your police scanner. When an accident or crime occurs, you will grab your high-quality camera, hop into the car, and head for the scene of the activity.

You will take photographs, perhaps two or three rolls worth, of everything and everybody in sight from every possible angle and will gather all of the names that you can.

Next you develop the film. Then you contact the accident or crime victim's attorney or insurance company and offer to sell your photographs. They will often be interested since you may have the only, or certainly the best, source of documented evidence available. You may be able to sell two, three, or four copies of your photographs to various interested parties, including the news media.

Earnings of well over a hundred dollars are possible from a single such photographic session. If you live in an active area, dozens of such opportunities may be present every week within a very small radius of your home.

Projectionist

IF YOU are a movie buff, here's a moonlighting opportunity to see every new release that hits town and get paid for it besides—as a *projectionist*.

The modern-day projectionist's activities have been simplified a great deal because many movie theaters have installed automated equipment. In a well-automated theater, the projectionist's activities may amount to only a few hours of specialized work per week per projector in addition to a rather casual supervision of equipment during the showing of a film.

One activity is to load the projector. Since a full-length movie comes on five to eight separate reels, they must be inspected and spliced together for use on platters, a large reel, or some other system. Next, the projector is threaded—and simple as that, it's show time! The projectionist flips on the switch, and if everything runs smoothly, that's the last activity until the movie is finished.

During the movie, the projectionist observes the equipment to see that everything is running properly. On rare occasions, the film may break or the projector might jam and an emergency splicing job or rethreading may be necessary. When the movie is finished, the film is rewound to get set for the next viewing.

After the movie's last showing, the film is once again separated into individual reels, packed up, and shipped back to the distributor.

If the theater has only one or two screens and automated equipment, the projectionist will probably not even need to be in the projection booth during the entire movie. This is because well-maintained automated projectors rarely break down and problems seldom develop. Therefore, the projectionist might also assist with crowd control, help operate the concession stand, or perform other miscellaneous duties.

If the theater does not have fully automated projectors, or if there are many films being shown at the same time on different screens (perhaps five or six), the projectionist may well be kept busy full time in the projection booth.

It is relatively easy to become a projectionist. The first requirement is to have a basic level of mechanical ability. The next thing is to acquire the specific skills you will perform, like loading the projector, operating the equipment, and making emergency repairs. This can be learned through on-the-job training by working with an experienced projectionist for a week or so. Therefore, if you have never operated a projector but would like to become a projectionist, you should not let your lack of experience or knowledge stop you. Your willingness to learn and your sincere interest will be persuasive enough to convince many theater managers that it will be worth the effort to train you.

Each theater may have its own way of operating a projection booth, and the specific equipment may vary somewhat. Nevertheless, there is a great deal of carry-over, and once you learn to become a projectionist, you can quickly adapt to equipment and procedures used at virtually any theater.

Movie-theater projectionists are ordinarily paid an hourly wage, which may range from minimum wage to two or three times that amount. Since the work is not usually demanding and long periods of time may pass without your doing anything but observation, the pay might be considered relatively high for the actual amount of work performed. Working conditions are usually pleasant, and part-time work shifts can be often arranged on a daily, nightly, weekend, or seasonal basis. There is virtually no investment required to become a projectionist, since you are providing a personal service.

In addition to being an employee of a theater, other possibilities exist to be a *free-lance projectionist* for *private screenings*. This might include operating projection equipment for a convention center or for a business during a sales meeting, annual meeting, or other event. Wealthy individuals with a projection room at home and advertising agencies are others that might be able to use your professional services.

You can land these accounts by making personal contacts or by sending out direct-mail pieces describing your professional service. Emphasize the benefits that they will receive from hiring you—a smooth, trouble-free viewing that does not cause them delays or embarrassment.

If you like the idea of working at a movie theater, but are not mechanically inclined, good part-time job possibilities exist as a *ticket seller*, *ticket taker*, *usher*, or *concession-stand operator*.

Promoter

Aʀᴇ ʏᴏᴜ the type of person who can make things happen? If so, the ideal way for you to moonlight may be as a *promoter*.

Perhaps the image that many people have of a promoter is someone who lines up boxing matches. Well, that is an accurate impression, but promoters can and do sponsor many other types of events as well. Musical concerts, flea markets, swap meets, and coin shows are just a few events that are ideal for a promoter's talents.

Primarily, a promoter is an organizer. If you are promoting a musical concert, for example, you will rent a concert hall or auditorium, hire the musical acts, advertise the event, and sell tickets to the concertgoers. A professional wrestling match would be handled in the same way. If you sponsor a flea market, swap meet, or similar event, you will rent a facility and advertise widely to attract exhibitors. You will then publicize the event to attract viewers and potential buyers of the exhibitors' goods. Most likely, you will charge each exhibitor an exhibitor's fee and will charge each viewer an admission fee.

Several factors will have great influence on your success or failure as a promoter. First, you must select an event that people will want to attend and for which they will pay money. Second, you must select an appropriate location, one that is in character with the activity and is accessible to your potential customers. Next, the event must be promoted and advertised widely enough so that all potential patrons are made aware of it and are enticed to attend. Then too, the event must be run smoothly so that patrons and others involved will feel it was worth their time, money, and effort and will return the next time you sponsor a similar program.

Careful financial forecasting is necessary before you make any firm commitment to sponsor an event. All sources of income should be explored. These include exhibitor's fees, admissions, concession income, income from the sale of products like programs or T-shirts, and advertising income from the sale of space in a program or on advertising display boards. All costs must be estimated, including facility rental, licenses, permits, advertising, insurance, and labor. If it appears that the event has a good chance for success, you can then continue with your plans. If it doesn't "pencil out," you will know in advance that the project is doomed to financial failure and you should explore other possibilities.

Special attention should be given to any state, county, or local regulations pertaining to sponsoring an event that draws a large number of persons. Often, health, safety, and crowd-control regulations must be met. This might include providing adequate rest-room facilities (particularly if the event is held outdoors), having medical personnel and ambulances available, and hiring an adequate number of security guards.

Check with your county recorder and city clerk to determine if a license or permit is required to sponsor an event. Also, you should obtain liability insurance to protect yourself in case a patron or participant becomes injured.

The primary requirements to operate as a promoter are ideas, organizational ability, time, and money. You will need an office from which you can operate (a home office is fine), and will need a telephone for business calls.

The amount of income you can earn from promoting a particular event can vary a great deal depending upon the circumstances and conditions. If you have chosen a popular attraction, selected a good location, picked a date free from strong competition and conflicts, promoted well, controlled your costs, and lucked out with ideal weather conditions, you can make a small fortune from a single event. If, however, your planning is faulty or you incur the ill winds of fate, you can conceivably suffer a substantial loss. Essentially, if you stick with events with which you are familiar and start out small, you can minimize your risks and maximize your chances of success.

Being a promoter can be the ideal way to moonlight for the person who wants to put forth concentrated effort on a specific, rather short-term project instead of working at a steady part-time job year round. You can easily control the amount of time involved by the number of events you sponsor. You might promote a series of concerts or meets or you could offer only one annual extravaganza that everyone in the community, county, or state looks forward to each year.

If the general idea of promoting appeals to you, but sporting events, musical concerts, and the like do not, you might consider becoming a *seminar promoter*. Here, you would follow the same principles and procedures as described above, but you would present seminars on topics such as how to stop smoking, natural childbirth, estate taxes, personality development, or any other subject in which people might be interested.

You would hire an author, professor, or someone with successful experience in some field to be the presenter, rent an auditorium or lecture hall, and advertise the event. Either locally or regionally known "experts" can be used, and you may be able to work your way up to sponsoring seminars with nationally known personalities.

State recertification laws in various professions like insurance, real estate, accounting, and cosmetology can provide you with a built-in clientele. This is because people in these areas must obtain a certain amount of continuing education before their licenses can be renewed. You will need to check with the state agency that controls an area in which you have an interest, since all courses must be approved before they will count for recertification.

Property Manager

Every real estate salesperson in the country has probably been faced with the same dilemma: a bona fide customer who wanted to buy investment rental property, who could afford to buy it, who knew that he or she should buy it—but then didn't buy it. What held that person back? Probably one thing—the time and requirements of managing the property. This situation reveals an outstanding opportunity to earn money part-time—as a *property manager*.

As a property manager, you will do as the title implies— manage property for the owner. You might be employed by one large investor or you might have many small property owners as clients. The scope of your activities might be broad or limited. Functions that you might perform include advertising property for rent, showing property to prospective tenants, leasing the property, collecting rents, and evicting tenants. You might also arrange for insurance on the property, pay bills, and supervise maintenance, repairs, landscaping, snow removal, and anything else that needs to be done. Your contract with the property owner, which should be in writing, will determine your responsibilities and authority.

There are many different types of real estate, including residential, commercial, shopping centers, agricultural, and special purpose for which your service is ideal. Since management of each type of property requires special skill and knowledge, it is probably best to concentrate in one area.

Attributes necessary to become a successful property manager include knowledge of property values and the rents they can command and an understanding of lease arrangements. You must also possess good human relations skills, since you may occasionally need to calm an irritated tenant, settle tenant disputes, and deal with plumbers, electricians, real estate agents, and others in the business world.

Licensing requirements for property managers vary from state to state. In many cases, particularly if you manage only a limited number of properties, no license is required. In other cases, a real estate license may be necessary. Contact the Real Estate Commission in your state to determine exactly what laws apply. Even though a real estate or property manager's license is not mandatory, you may find it beneficial to obtain one. Information learned in your study for the examination will be very helpful, and being licensed may assist you in obtaining more customers and a better class of clientele. Having a license may also earn you the recognition and approval of real estate agents, who will refer clients to you.

The periods of time you devote to being a property manager might best be described as sporadic. Days or even weeks may go by with very few or no occurrences which need your attention. On the other hand, you may get a phone call from a tenant at 2:00 A.M. saying a water pipe has burst, and you must spring into immediate action. The type of property, number of units, and property's condition will dictate to a large extent the amount of supervision that will be required of you.

Very little investment is required to become a property manager. You will need a telephone in your home that is always available to receive business calls and you will need a vehicle for transportation.

Property managers are paid a flat fee per unit each month

or receive a percentage of the gross rents collected. As an indication of the earnings potential, handling a dozen average-sized single residential units should earn you several hundred dollars per month. You can easily adjust your earnings and the amount of time required of you by changing the number of units you accept for management.

If you are a renter rather than an owner, you might look for an apartment building where you can become the live-in *apartment-complex manager.* In return for acting as manager, you will receive free rent, or at least a substantial decrease in your cost.

Real estate sales is another related occupation that should not be overlooked as a part-time activity. This is particularly true if you are required to obtain a real estate license in your state to become a property manager. Even if you do not actively pursue real estate sales, you may be able to refer prospective buyers and sellers to a cooperating real estate agent, for which you will receive a handsome referral fee.

Property Security Service

ARE THERE people in your community who leave their homes vacant for extended time periods while they take vacations or business trips? Undoubtedly there are. Besides traveling, these people most likely have one other factor in common: they worry a lot—about what's happening to their homes while they're gone, that is. Well, you can eliminate these worries and earn a good moonlighter's income for yourself at the same time—by operating a *property security service.*

The primary function of your property security service is to ensure that no vandalism, theft, or undue damage because of the elements occurs to the property while the owner is away. On a regular basis, perhaps daily, you will check the property. Examine the home's interior to see that pilot lights are lit, the furnace is operating, no water pipes have burst, and that all windows and doors are securely locked. Check the exterior for potential problems, such as a broken tree limb that is about to fall on the house, and for damage caused by weather conditions. If something needs immediate repair, you should get it fixed if you are authorized to do so, exercising good judgment in buying materials and hiring repairmen.

You might also offer additional services such as watering plants and collecting the mail.

Since it is the well-to-do who can most easily afford the time and money to travel, they will constitute the bulk of your clientele. Advertising in the newsletters of country clubs, yacht clubs, and the chamber of commerce is an ideal way to contact them. You might also use direct mail, sending letters to persons you can identify as good potential clients. Advertisements in the travel section of your local newspapers should also reach many who will find your service of interest.

If you live in a summer or winter vacation area, there are many potential clients for your service, since many vacationers probably own a home that is used for their seasonal vacation only. You might make door-to-door calls to explain your service or use direct mail to all persons in the telephone directory who have an address that appears as though it could belong to a part-time resident. Your chamber of commerce may offer a "criss-cross" directory, which lists properties by address, or may be able to tell you how to obtain one. Also, inform all area real estate agents of your service and leave some of your business cards with them. They will be happy to relay the information to prospective vacation-home buyers, since it may help them in closing a sale.

Lending institutions, which often have vacant homes that were repossessed, can also be good clients.

The primary qualities you will need to operate your property security service are the intangibles of dependability, honesty, and integrity. If you promise to check the home daily, then you must do so. You must not rummage through your client's closets, dressers, and other personal possessions, and you must keep your clients' personal and business affairs strictly confidential.

Very little investment is necessary to establish your property security service. You will need a suitable vehicle to make your rounds and will need a telephone in your home that is available for business calls. Small expenditures will be required for advertising and to have business cards printed.

Set the charge for your service at a weekly or monthly rate, based upon the number of property inspections you must make and the amount of time required for each. Base your fee on a suitable rate per hour, say at two to four times the minimum wage rate.

Since you will have contacts with many persons whose homes are often unattended, a natural activity for you to offer these same clients is a *lawn and landscape service*. Here, you would mow lawns, trim hedges, and, in general, care for the grounds.

Publicity Agent

Can you turn a molehill into a mountain? Could you make a shopping trip to your local grocery store sound like an excursion on the Riviera? Do you like telling people about some upcoming event that you're excited about? If these thought-provoking questions have raised your curiosity, perhaps you should consider moonlighting as a *publicity agent*.

To set the record straight, publicity agents don't actually turn molehills into mountains or make ordinary shopping trips sound like glamorous European vacations. What they do, however, is sometimes quite similar—they promote and publicize their client's proposition in as favorable a light as possible. A good publicity agent does this by making the proposition sound exciting, interesting, enticing, tantalizing, and too good to pass by—all within the boundaries of good taste and truthfulness.

The publicity agent might prepare news releases, arrange news conferences, stage special promotional activities like giveaways or rebates, organize contests, or develop and mail out brochures and newsletters. Other activities might include organizing marketing research or telephone surveys, planning seminars, preparing advertising, and doing just about anything that isn't illegal or immoral to promote the client's proposition. Primarily, a publicity agent is an "idea" person who creates ways to publicize the proposition and who then develops techniques for carrying those ideas through to completion.

No particular training or certification is necessary to become a publicity agent, but a background in advertising, psychology, sociology, and communications would be helpful. As important as formal training are imagination, creativity, a penchant for detail, thorough follow-through, and, perhaps, a sense of daring. Artistic skills may be helpful, and a knowledge of all available publicity channels and media is necessary. Often, the publicity agent contracts for services of experts or specialists when unique skills are needed.

There are many possibilities for you to ply your skills as a publicity agent on a part-time basis. One, of course, is to work for an established public relations company, publicity agent, or advertising agency. In this position, you will be an employee working on accounts that are established by your employer. Another possibility is to work as an employee for one specific company. Here, you might handle special promotional events or work on some phase of a major promotional program.

A third opportunity, and perhaps the one that is most exciting, is to operate your own publicity agency. Here, you will handle promotions and publicity for various clients on a freelance basis. Obviously, if you work part-time at this activity, you will not have the time, resources, contacts, or staff to handle major accounts. Your clientele, at least initially, will be quite different. They will be individuals, organizations, and small businesses that either cannot afford a large publicity agency's services or would not feel comfortable in using one. This includes musical groups, authors, songwriters, home businesses, specialty retail shops, service organizations, churches, schools, and all sorts of small businesses like nightclubs, restaurants, and furniture dealers. You might develop a promotional program for one special event or you could handle your client's publicity and promotions on an ongoing basis.

Your first client is easy to locate—it is *you*. You can demonstrate your promotional skills by devising a well-organized and perhaps unique or eye-catching way to inform prospective customers of your service. Perhaps business cards of unusual size or design, individual announcements hand-delivered by you in unusual dress, or use of a video tape will attract attention without distracting from your goal—landing a client. If your approach is different, tasteful, and functional, you will have more clients in short order than you can possibly handle.

Since a publicity agent primarily provides a service—that is, the development of a promotional package—you will have little investment in equipment and supplies. You will probably need to have access to a typewriter and copy machine or duplicator and will need a telephone for business purposes. Since you work part time, you can easily operate out of your home or, if you wish, you can establish a small office in a business location.

You will pay your own costs and expenses for items like paper supplies and long-distance phone charges. Your client will pay for printing charges, advertising expenses, and any other costs for materials or publicity connected with the promotional program. The scope of your authority should be identified and a budget drafted with your client before you start on the program.

Most likely, your clients will want an estimate of your fee before they engage your services. Carefully estimate the amount of time you will need and any costs you might incur personally. The hourly rate you can charge will depend upon your experience and proven successes. It will be easy to raise your rates after you have developed a portfolio of success stories to display to prospective clients.

If you land a big account or develop more regular customers than you can handle, you can hire other creative moonlighters to help you. This might be a great time to specialize by bringing artists, ad writers, communication experts, and others on board to handle specific tasks on a part-time basis when needed.

If you like to be where the action is, being a publicity agent is probably ideal for you. It will give you an opportunity to vent your creative talents, to help your clients achieve their goals, and to make a substantial income as well.

Another possibility is to operate an *ad-writing service*. Here, you would specialize in preparing advertising copy and advertising campaigns for one or more small clients who cannot afford the services of a larger, professional advertising agency.

Real Estate Sales

At what price does the average home in your community sell—$60,000, $80,000, $100,000, $120,000, higher? What is the commission rate charged by real estate agents—6, 7, 8 percent? If we combine the answers to these two questions, we find another answer—that is, why so many people nationwide moonlight in *real estate sales*. There's *money* in it, lots of money.

While we're on the topic of money, let's calculate how much a part-time real estate salesperson can earn from the sale of a single, average-priced house. Certainly, real estate property values vary throughout the country and real estate commission rates also vary, often from agency to agency in the same community.

For our purposes (for ease of calculation), let's select $100,000 as the sales price and 7 percent as the commission rate.

Before we hastily calculate the salesperson's earnings, it is necessary to know a little more about how the commission will be divided between the parties involved. Actually, the commission consists of two parts—that for *listing* the property for sale and that for *selling* the property. If one real estate agency listed the property (that is, got the owner to sign a listing agreement, placing the property for sale), that agency gets the listing portion of the commission. If another agency sold the property, that agency gets the selling portion of the commission. If the same agency both listed and sold a property, it gets both parts, or the full commission.

The division of commission between listing agency and selling agency is set by agreement between the agencies involved, and no universal split exists. Arrangements of 40-60 or 50-50, with the lister's share shown first, are fairly common, however.

In our example, let's assume our salesperson's sale is of another agency's listing and that a 50-50 commission split between lister and seller is in effect. The commission would therefore be calculated as follows:

Sales price:	$100,000
Commission rate:	7%
Total commission:	$7,000

Division of $7,000 commission: 50% to listing agency: $3,500
50% to selling agency: $3,500

So, did our salesperson earn $3,500? Not so fast. A real estate salesperson is not self-employed. He or she works through a real estate broker (an agency). Ordinarily the broker provides the salesperson's office space and pays all advertising, utilities, and other office expenses. In return, the broker shares in whatever the real estate salesperson earns in commissions, often on a 50-50 split. Therefore, of the $3,500 earned by the selling agency from the salesperson's sale, the broker gets half, or $1,750, and the salesperson receives the other $1,750.

It's not fair, you say. The salesperson should get more. Well, keep in mind that often another agent will sell one of this salesperson's listings, and then this salesperson will receive a substantial listing commission. Also, there will be many cases where this salesperson will sell one of his or her own listings and receive double the commission shown here, or $3,500.

This rather lengthy example is presented to demonstrate two principles of the real estate business: how real estate commissions are calculated and that there are two attractive ways to earn money—by listing property and by selling it.

Since the real estate business can be very lucrative, many people enter this field, and the competition is stiff. Therefore, it is necessary to possess adequate skills if you are to become successful. Paramount of these is the ability to *prospect*—that is, to find customers who are willing to sell or buy real estate. Thorough follow-up is also necessary, since you must often keep in touch with your prospects and keep them "warm" for many weeks or months until their circumstances and attitudes are right to proceed with the transaction. In addition to these salesmanship skills, a thorough background in real estate terminology, principles, and procedures is necessary.

All states require that real estate salespeople be licensed. The specifics vary from state to state, but it ordinarily consists of passing a single exam administered by the state Real Estate Commission. Some states require a limited amount of real estate education before, or after, taking the exam. Check with your state Real Estate Commission to determine what will be required of you to become licensed. Ordinarily, a single course in real estate principles and self study, or thorough self study alone, will be adequate to enable you to pass the real estate exam and enter the real estate profession.

Very little investment is required to enter real estate sales. You will need a suitable automobile, appropriate clothing to look the part, and a few miscellaneous supplies. The real estate exam and license fees are low—usually in the $10 to $30 range.

Since real estate salespeople work for real estate brokers, it is necessary that you find a broker to "hire" you before you can begin. Your background, appearance, honesty, sincerity, and determination will be among your best references. Real estate brokers are almost always willing to add another person possessing those skills to their staff.

Real estate brokers and salespeople handle many types of property, including residential, commercial, agricultural, building sites, and special-use properties. Since each of these requires a certain degree of specialized knowledge, it might be best to concentrate on one or two areas.

An active and aggressive part-time real estate salesperson can earn a substantial amount of money. In fact, if you list and sell just two average-size properties per month, your earnings will exceed what many people make at a full-time job, perhaps yourself included.

Since you will often deal with your customers by appointment, you can control your time schedule quite well in the real estate business. Often, if one of your clients needs attention while you are at your regular job, your broker will cover for you as part of his or her office responsibilities.

A related area you might expand into once you have gained experience in the real estate field is that of *certified real estate appraiser*. Here, you would determine the market value of real estate after a thorough review and study of all aspects pertaining to the property's value. Additional training beyond the real estate salesperson's or broker's license is ordinarily required to become a certified appraiser.

If you have lots of contacts who would make good prospects but don't want to become actively involved in real estate sales, you may be able to work with a broker on a *referral basis* only. Here, you will furnish high-quality names to the broker, who will pay you a referral fee, of say 10 to 20 percent of whatever is earned from dealings with those prospects. Since you will be earning a commission from your activities, it is necessary for you to be licensed in order to work on a referral basis.

Real estate sales can be one of the most lucrative, prestigious, and exciting of all moonlighting activities. Even though some effort is necessary to become licensed, very few professions offering this much potential are this easy to enter.

Recreation Director

Do you like fun and games? Do you have a flair for organization? If you answered yes to both of these questions, you should consider moonlighting as a *recreation director*.

As a recreation director, you will organize activities where other people can have fun. This might include organizing volleyball games, softball games, hikes, camping trips, ski parties, boat rides, dances, trail rides, swimming parties, and the like.

You might organize and supervise regular leagues in bowling, racquetball, golf, tennis, softball, or horseshoes. Perhaps you will set up tournaments in these areas or in bridge, billiards, or backgammon.

Providing a children's storybook hour, arts and crafts classes, feature-length movies, tours of museums or historical sites, or arranging for guest speakers might also fall within the broad range of activities you offer.

Offer—for whom? Many possibilities exist. In general, these are businesses or institutions that cannot afford to hire a full-time recreation director but yet need someone to perform this function. In other cases, organizations with a full-time recreation director, and perhaps even a staff, may need additional assistance. These include hotels, resorts, campgrounds, physical-fitness centers, churches, health spas, and all types of private clubs, lodges, and country clubs. Colleges, public school systems, and private schools that offer intramural programs are also good possibilities.

Large businesses, with enough employees to support such a program, also often organize their own leagues or recreational activities. Youth camps, retreats, and summer youth programs are also good potential users of your services. In addition, city-sponsored recreation programs offer much potential. Then too, the elderly should not be overlooked. Nursing homes and area government agencies, like the Agency on Aging, may well be able to use a part-time recreation director.

Exactly what your function will be as a recreation director can vary immensely. In some cases, it will be primarily organizational, where you make arrangements for the activities and select people to supervise them. In others, you might perform all organizational and supervisory activities yourself. The size of the organization, number of activities, number of participants, and budget will largely dictate what your activities will be, or must be.

Qualities required to become a successful recreation director include organizational abilities and leadership skills. You must plan each activity well in advance, publicize it, and encourage people to participate. Facilities must be reserved and arrangements double-checked to be certain they will be available when needed. All equipment, supplies, and materials must be on hand and in proper working order. Supervisory personnel, assistants, and officiators need to be contacted and must be on hand and ready to go on time. Creativity, imagination, and ingenuity are also desirable traits to be able to call upon when things don't go as planned.

In some cases, a thorough technical knowledge of the games and activities provided is necessary; in others, it is not. This depends upon the amount of direct contact you have with the actual presentation and supervision of the activity. Obviously, if you are to teach others how to do something, or if you are a referee or umpire, you must know the activity well. If your activities are primarily organizational, this in-depth knowledge is not necessary. Still, you will need to know enough about each activity to schedule the proper number of participants and supervisors and to provide an adequate amount of time, supplies, and equipment for the activity.

Virtually no investment in materials, equipment, supplies, or anything else is required to become a recreation director, since you are providing a personal service. Usually, no licensing or certification is required either. If you are to be employed by a school system, however, you should check with your State Department of Education. Likewise, if you will be working with the elderly, you might check with the Social Services Department.

Your pay for serving as a recreation director may be at an hourly rate, say two to four times the minimum wage rate, or it might be a flat amount for organizing and supervising a league or tournament.

This can be the ideal moonlighting activity for former high school and college athletes and for those currently involved in the coaching profession. In addition to earning the supplementary money you require, you can also keep in physical shape and have a lot of fun by participating in the activities yourself.

Related areas where you can utilize your interest in recreational activities and your organizational abilities include offering *private or group lessons*, operating a *sports clinic*, operating a *sports camp*, or becoming a *sports official*. You can also specialize as a *tournament organizer*, where you plan, promote, and supervise golf, bowling, tennis, or other tournaments for area businesses, clubs, or organizations.

Recycling

If you are both ecologically and economically oriented, *recycling* may be the perfect way for you to moonlight.

As a recycler, you will collect various materials that have served their purpose and sell them, primarily to a recycling center. The recycling center amasses a large quantity of the material and sells it to a manufacturer or processor. The material is then processed, returning it more or less to its raw-material state. It is then used for manufacturing products that are sold to consumers. Companies prefer to recycle materials because it is often less costly than processing raw materials and because it helps conserve natural resources.

Various metals, including copper, brass, steel, aluminum, cast iron, stainless steel, and lead are suitable for sale to either a recycling center or junk dealer. These dealers ordinarily require that the various types of metal be separated, so you will need to learn how to identify each by color, weight, magnetic qualities, and usage. With a little experience, you will quickly become an expert at this.

Metals can be located at a variety of sources, including construction sites and farm groves, where you may even get paid for cleaning up the area. Rural or small-town dump grounds are other possibilities. Often too, good buys can be made at auctions of what seems to be worthless or broken-down equipment but which has salvage value for the metal content. Dead batteries from vehicles are also good items for recycling, since they contain lead.

Paper is another commodity that can be sold, by the ton, to recycling centers. The price varies with the grade of paper, with high-quality writing paper and computer printouts being among the better paying. Corrugated paper (cardboard boxes) and newspaper are lower grade and therefore poorer paying. Recycling centers often refuse to accept magazines because of the nonsoluble glue used in some bindings.

Insulation manufacturing companies that make cellulose insulation from paper are also good potential buyers for you to contact.

Because a large volume is necessary to make collecting paper for recycling a feasible activity, business and industry are usually the best sources. In cities, where the prices charged for garbage collection are high, you can probably locate many businesses that will give you their paper if you will haul it away, and some of them may even pay you for doing so.

Fabrics, which are recycled as carpeting, blankets, apparel, and building materials, can also be a good product to handle. As with collecting paper, business and industry will most likely be your best source to obtain a sizable quantity.

Used tires and other rubber products are ground up and recycled in roofing and siding materials, asphalt paving, hosing, and other products. Another way to recycle used tires is to sell them to tire-retreading companies. Used tires can often be obtained from service stations free of charge.

Collecting materials for sale to recycling centers can frequently go hand in hand with another activity, like operating a garbage collection route or being an auctioneer.

The market for metals, paper, and other recyclable materials is volatile and cyclical. Prices may range widely during the year from very acceptably high amounts to those that are so low that it would not appear to be worth your while collecting the goods. In fact, there may be times when dealers refuse to buy a particular commodity at all. Therefore, it is ideal to have storage space available where you can accumulate materials until the demand returns and prices once again reach acceptable levels.

Before you start collecting anything, you should first become familiar with the recycling dealers in your area to determine what type of materials they accept. Most of these dealers are specialized, handling only one or two types of goods, and it may be possible that no one in your area handles a product like fabrics or paper.

About the only equipment you need to operate your recycling business is a vehicle for hauling the materials. A pickup truck or van is ideal, but a two-wheel trailer can also be serviceable.

The amount of income you can earn by recycling materials will vary depending upon how hard you work at it and the current level of prices. Since the prices vary from time to time and from dealer to dealer, you can increase your income by carefully studying the market and by shopping around for the dealer who pays the highest price on each type of goods you have for sale. On the average, you should be able to easily earn several hundred dollars per month by devoting a portion of your spare time to this moonlighting activity. One of the fun things about recycling is that, in effect, you *can* get something for nothing, since much of what you sell will be given to you for free— or you may even be paid to cart it away!

Another job possibility in recycling is as a *used-lumber dealer*. Many people will give away or sell inexpensively an old house, barn, or shed that they want removed from the premises. These old structures often contain a small fortune in good-quality, full-dimension lumber that can be sold or used in your own building projects. Any wood scraps or broken pieces that cannot be sold for lumber can be sold for firewood or used for that purpose yourself.

In addition, there is often a large quantity of copper pipe, wire, nails, bolts, and other metal that has good sales value at a recycling center. Then, to add a little excitement, suspense, and anticipation to this recycling opportunity, there is always the chance that you will stumble across a real "find" in the attic or walls of an old house.

A final idea is to recycle used automobile parts by operating an *automobile salvage yard*. Here, you would buy (or receive free for hauling them away) vehicles wrecked in accidents or those that no longer run. You would strip them of any good, usable parts. Thereafter, in effect, your operation becomes a used-auto-parts store. The parts can usually be sold to body shops and auto repair shops at one-fourth to one-half the price of new parts. Those portions of the vehicle that cannot be sold for parts can be sold as scrap metal to a recycling center.

Repair Service

WHEN A product stops working properly or breaks down altogether, there are three choices available: (1.) Throw it out and buy new; (2.) Keep using it until it has given its last ounce of service, and then throw it out; (3.) Have it restored to good, workable condition. Often, it is this third choice that is selected by many people, which is why operating a *repair service* is a worthwhile moonlighting activity to consider.

Almost any type of product that has a fairly high replacement cost or that might have a sentimental value can be ideal for your repair talents. This includes bicycles, lawn mowers, automobile radios and tape players, garden tractors, motorcycles, watches, appliances, guns, snowmobiles, sports equipment, shoes, door chimes, and antiques.

You might deal in *vinyl repair*, where you regularly call on used-auto dealers and upholstery shops. Another good area is *mobile-home repair*, where you install skirting and make exterior wall and roof improvements. You might choose a highly spec-ialized area like *photograph restoration* or *doll repair* and become the "expert" that everyone for miles around seeks out. There are hundreds, if not thousands, of good product areas for you to consider.

Many of your customers will be individuals. You might also be able to work out an arrangement with one or more local businesses where you subcontract to fix items brought in by their customers for repair.

If you already have knowledge of how to make repairs in your chosen area, you are ready to start. If not, you will need to learn before hanging out your shingle. The type of items you repair will largely dictate the amount and type of training required. In many cases, you can learn through experimentation and practice. In others, you may need to take a specialized course or program of study from an area vocational-technical school, specialized institute, or correspondence school.

The amount of equipment needed to operate your repair service, and its cost, will depend upon the type of products you repair. Likewise, the amount and cost of your inventory of replacement parts will vary a great deal. In some cases, a total investment of less than a hundred dollars may set you up nicely, while thousands of dollars will be required to equip other repair shops. Investigate what your total investment cost will be before you get too far along in your planning.

Usually, no special certification or licensing is necessary, other than perhaps a city or county permit, to operate a repair service. In some cases, it is possible to become "certified" by attending a course of instruction or series of seminars. This designation may be well worth the effort, since having it will lend a great deal of credibility to your service. This can be a powerful tool in advertising and sales promotion, resulting in more customers and higher fees.

As a repair service operator, you are a businessperson, and everything you do should be according to well-established business principles. Your service will be judged upon three factors: your ability to repair the product right the first time, the speed with which you repair items and whether or not you have work finished when promised, and your prices. The importance of these, to most customers, is probably in the order listed.

You can operate your repair service from a home workshop, a commercial business location, or, if appropriate, a well-equipped van or truck. Another possibility is to work as an employee for an established repair shop.

Set your hourly labor rate to be in line with that charged by others in your area. This will vary from one type of repair work to another, with a general range of two to five times the minimum wage rate. Charge regular retail prices for all replacement parts, materials, and supplies. Since you will buy these items at discount wholesale prices from manufacturers and suppliers, you will make a profit on each item sold.

Repairing and restoring broken and beaten items can be wonderfully satisfying work. It can be a particularly attractive way to moonlight for people who like to visually witness the results of their labors.

A natural extension of the repair service is to become a dealer in your area of specialization. You can operate a regular retail outlet whereby you buy new merchandise from manufacturers and suppliers or you can deal in used merchandise that you have acquired and restored to salable condition.

Sewing

I𝐹 you are a whiz with needle and thread, you can make your moonlighting money by sewing. Several good possibilities exist in this area, and you can be kept as busy as you want in any one of them or you can add to your enjoyment by engaging in them all.

Clothing alteration is usually one of the steadiest of all part-time pursuits. Here, you will increase or decrease the waistline in slacks or skirts, lengthen or shorten garments, remove or add cuffs or lapels, replace buttons and zippers, and make other changes in style and fit.

In addition to individuals, small clothing stores that cannot afford someone full time to make alterations may be able to use your services. If you offer to pick up garments and return them within a day or two, you should have no difficulty landing one or two accounts that will keep you very busy.

Set your rates according to what others in your area charge for similar services and based upon what customers are willing to pay. The rate charged and your efficiency and expertise will determine your earnings per hour, but two to four times the minimum wage rate will probably be the general range you can expect.

Tailoring is another viable way to earn money part time with your sewing machine. Here, you will sew garments to special order for clients who either prefer styles and materials not available at clothing stores or who cannot get a decent fit with garments off a clothier's rack. Your clients may include those who want extra-high quality in materials and workmanship or those who want to look unique and individualistic.

Garments individually sewn to special measurements using hand-selected materials will be more costly than mass-produced goods available from a clothing store. Therefore, your clients will most likely consist of the well-to-do and those of exceptional taste and requirements. They will expect your work to be flawless—but they will also pay you well for your efforts. A single garment may cost hundreds, or even thousands, of dollars.

Since your work is specialized, high quality, and demanding, your earnings should be high. Do not be bashful in quoting prices that will pay you well for your efforts.

Clothing design and manufacture is another avenue you might pursue. As the term suggests, you would design clothing and manufacture it. Then, you would sell it to someone, probably a retailer. Since individually sewn garments will require a good deal of time, this activity can be successful as a small-scale operation only if you deal in unique, one-of-a-kind garments that sell at high prices in exclusive shops. Low-priced garments would not yield enough profit to pay you an adequate hourly income for your time.

To be successful in this competitive field, your designs must be unique and appealing, your selection of fabrics, other materials, and colors must be tasteful, and your craftsmanship must be extraordinary. All this must be combined with a knowledge of the fashion market and an awareness of buyers' interest and needs.

You might start by designing and sewing a few garments. You can then contact carefully selected clothiers who deal in similar quality and style of goods. If the clothier will not buy your creations outright, you might offer to place them in the store on consignment. Under this arrangement, you will not be paid until the garment sells. Many clothiers will find your confidence in your product and your willingness to share the risk refreshing. You should, therefore, have no difficulty finding merchants to give you a chance to market your wares under this plan. Once your garments prove their marketability, you can expand your production and the number of outlets that handle your goods.

Your earnings per garment sold can be high, since each item may well sell for several hundred, or perhaps even thousands, of dollars. If your designs are truly original, you may be able to sell them to a clothing manufacturer or you may be able to expand your own operation.

If you do a good job at any one of the sewing activities described here, it is entirely possible, even likely, that you will soon be overrun with more business than you can handle. You can then increase your production, and your income, by hiring others, who are well qualified, to help you.

If the idea of earning money part time by sewing appeals to you, the investment to get started may be minimal. This is because you probably already have the sewing machine, scissors, thimbles, needles, pins, and other miscellaneous equipment and supplies you will need. If you do not have a high-quality sewing machine, you should get one. You will also need thread in various thicknesses and colors and you should stock standard buttons, zippers, snaps, and hooks. All in all, even if you must buy all the equipment and supplies to get started, the investment will be relatively small.

Your earnings will vary with the type of sewing activity you pursue and the amount of time you devote to it. Several hundred dollars per month is easily within reach, and you can earn considerably more if you care to put forth extra effort or hire assistants.

If you like the sewing area but prefer to work with bigger items than clothing, you might operate a *canvas repair shop*. Here, you would repair boat tops, store awnings, automobile convertible tops, and all sorts of canvas products. You might even manufacture these items to special order.

You might also consider operating a *drapery service*, where you would sew custom-made curtains and drapes and perhaps install them.

Speculator

HERE's a moonlighting activity that is *not* for the faint of heart, but it is for the aggressive, wheeler-dealer type who is willing to take a risk—being a *speculator*.

A speculator is one who enters some type of high-risk investment with the expectation (hope!) of making a substantial profit on the transaction, usually in a short time period.

Contrary to what many people might believe, a speculator is *not* a gambler. A gambler enters a high-risk proposition with little or no study or background—everything is pretty well left to chance. A speculator, on the other hand, enters a high-risk proposition with a great deal of study and background knowledge, recognizing and understanding full well all the potential risks and rewards involved. In other words, much time and effort is required to become a true speculator. That is why it is included as a way to moonlight.

A person can speculate in almost anything, but real estate and the futures market are often the two most appealing areas. This is because the speculator can obtain a great deal of *leverage* in these mediums. This means that speculators put up relatively little of their own cash and primarily use other people's funds to control the investment. For example, in the real estate area, a 25 percent down payment may be required to buy an invest-ment property. Thus, if the purchase price is $100,000, the speculator puts up only $25,000, uses $75,000 of someone else's funds (from a lending institution, usually), and controls the en-tire $100,000 property.

This use of leverage gives the opportunity for a fantastic rate of return on the investment. Assume, for example, that the $100,000 property increases in value 15 percent in the first year. This will be a $15,000 increase ($100,000 x 15% = $15,000) on a cash investment of $25,000, or a 60 percent annual rate of return.

Often, a speculator tries to purchase real estate with little or no cash investment. This is sometimes possible if a seller is des-perate and willing to negotiate terms, any terms, to get rid of the property. In essence, the speculator borrows from a lending institution as much of the purchase price as possible and gives that to the seller. Instead of giving the seller the remaining amount as a cash down payment, the speculator gives the seller a *promissory note*—that is, a promise to pay the money at some specific date in the future. This may call for monthly or quarterly payments over several years or it may call for a lump sum (bal-loon) payment one, three, or five years hence.

In most cases, sellers of high-quality property do not need to resort to accepting these terms to unload their holdings. Therefore, it is often poorer-quality property on which these terms are available. Many times, the speculator buys the property with the intention of refurbishing it, thus increasing its value, and then selling it at a substantial profit.

Many of the "get-rich-quick" ideas advertised in magazines, newspapers, and tabloids are based on the theory of *real estate pyramiding*. This is a technique whereby the investor acquires one property and increases its value substantially through making relatively inexpensive improvements or by changing its use to something more profitable. Then, the equity (amount of owner's value) in that property is pledged as security to borrow the down payment to buy another similar property, where improvements are made and value is increased. The equity in that property is used to acquire another, and so on. This chain reaction continues until the speculator has acquired many valuable properties, all from a beginning of very little, or no, cash investment.

In theory, real estate pyramiding works to perfection. In practice, however, ideal economic conditions, a keen sense of the real estate market, and shrewd business acumen are necessary to achieve even modest success. In other words, this is a technique that should not be tried by just anyone.

A thorough background in real estate financing and procedures should be developed before becoming a real estate speculator. Many books are available on the topic, and seminars and workshops are also worth attending.

Many commodities, including wheat, corn, soybeans, livestock, lumber, cocoa, coffee, cotton, orange juice, silver, and gold, are traded on the *futures market*. Trading is conducted in terms of *contracts* consisting of a certain number of pounds, ounces, board feet, and so on. For instance, a corn contract is 5,000 bushels, a lumber contract is 130,000 board feet, and a silver contract is 5,000 troy ounces. Contracts are bought or sold for delivery several months in the future. The speculator does not actually intend to take delivery of the commodity though and buys up the contract before its delivery date.

The value of a contract is determined by multiplying the

number of units in the contract times the price per unit. For example, there are 5,000 bushels of wheat in a contract. If the price of wheat is $4 per bushel, the value of a single contract is $20,000 (5,000 bushels x $4 = $20,000).

The feature that speculators find attractive about the futures market is that contracts can be acquired on *margin*—that is, by making a small down payment, say of perhaps 10 percent of the contract's value. Therefore, if the value of a wheat contract is $20,000 and the margin requirement is 10 percent, the speculator's cash outlay is only $2,000.

Commodity prices can vary widely in a single day. An increase or decrease of 10, 15, or 20 cents per bushel, for example, are not uncommon. Because of this, a speculator can make a fantastic return, or suffer a devastating loss, in a very short time period, maybe in only a few hours, days, or weeks. For example, assume that in the morning a speculator buys a contract of wheat (5,000 bushels) at $4.00 per bushel, making a margin payment of $2,000. By day's end, the price is at $4.10 per bushel and the speculator sells. This seemingly small 10-cent price increase is on each of the 5,000 bushels, for a $500 profit in a single day, less brokerage fees of perhaps $50 to $75. This is a return of approximately 22.5 percent on the initial $2,000 investment. Since rates of return are always expressed in terms of a *year*, this amounts to a whopping annual percentage rate of 8,212.5 percent! Before enthusiasm carries you away and you rush out to buy a futures contract, keep in mind that if the price had dropped 10 cents per bushel, the *loss* would have been at the same 8,212.5 percent annual percentage rate.

The fact that a speculator can make a profit in the futures market if the price goes up *or* down, just as long as the proper prediction was made in advance, makes this area doubly exciting. The investment technique known as *selling short* is used to make a profit if prices decrease. This is an area that requires a lot of expertise, and amateurs should proceed very cautiously. For more information on the futures market, contact the Chicago

Merchantile Exchange, 444 West Jackson Boulevard, Chicago, IL 60606.

Opportunities for a speculator are not limited to real estate and the futures market. Antiques, common stocks, diamonds, and just about anything can be a possibility. The goal is always the same—to buy at a low price and to sell at a higher one, in a short time. Some speculators buy anything, regardless of what it is, if they feel they can make a quick profit on it.

It must be emphasized strongly that in order to be a true speculator, you must have a wealth of knowledge in the area in which you are dealing. Much study and analysis is required. Decisions must be based on fact and educated predictions rather than on guesses, rumors, or hunches. If being a speculator is appealing to you, choose one area and become an expert in it.

A speculator's primary investments are in cash and time. Cash to finance the dealings and time to carefully study and monitor them. If you are short on one of these, you might align yourself with a partner who possesses the missing quality.

A speculator's income potential can be phenomenal if the right decisions are made at the right time. Conversely, the losses can be just as large if poor decisions are made. A good rule of thumb is to never speculate with money you can't afford to lose.

For the right person of aggressive nature who craves action, speculation can be the most exciting way there is to moonlight; in fact, it may be the *only* acceptable way to moonlight!

Sports Officiating

"MOIDER DA BUM!" "You bush leaguer!" "You stink!" If you can withstand verbal abuse like this, often from a thousand people or more at a time, you've passed half of the sports officiating test already!

Many possibilities exist for plying your skills as a *sports offi-ciator*, including junior high school, high school, junior college, and college men's and women's activities. Contests in basketball, football, volleyball, gymnastics, swimming, tennis, baseball, and softball provide the opportunity to keep busy year round. Other possibilities exist for officiating games for the city recreation league, YMCA, YWCA, and any variety of recreation center or industrial league. In fact, if you are licensed to officiate several sports, you can probably keep busy every night of the week if you wish!

In order to officiate most types of contests, you must be licensed. Licensing for junior high and high school activities is administered by the State High School Athletic Association in each state. Although procedures vary somewhat from state to state, the primary requirement is that you pass a written exam on the rules of the game. Often, this exam is an open-book test, but it is rigorous and you must know where to find the rules in the book and know how to interpret them. Upon passing this test, in many states you become a *licensed official*, which allows you to officiate for a limited time period, say three years. After that, you take a closed-book test and upon passing it become a *certified official*. In most states, sports officials are required to attend an annual *rules meeting*, where new rules and procedures are explained and discussed.

Since separate licensing is required for each sport, most sports officiators stick to just one sport per season or get licensed in related activities such as both men's and women's basketball. Each license is renewable on an annual basis by submitting a minimal fee, usually in the $15 to $25 range.

After gaining experience as a junior high, high school, and recreation-league official, you may want to move into junior college and four-year-college officiating. In many states, no ad-ditional certification is required to officiate junior college con-tests. In order to officiate four-year college and university games, you must generally be certified by the National Collegiate Athletic Association (NCAA).

No particular licensing may be required to officiate contests in city recreation leagues and the like; however, licensing will help you obtain jobs and will give you the confidence necessary to do a good job.

Attributes that are necessary to become a successful sports officiator include good eyesight, sound judgment, and the ability to make quick decisions and the fortitude to stick with them. Poise in a pressure-packed situation, an even temperament, mental dexterity to quickly and accurately recall and apply the game's rules, and the physical stamina to keep up with the pace of the game are also required.

Once you are licensed, the next step is to line up contests to officiate. For some activities, officials work in crews of two or more persons, and the officiators are often hired as a crew rather than separately. This is because the sports officiators must often develop teamwork procedures and a philosophy for officiating a contest. Therefore, it may be necessary to align yourself with one or more partners with whom you can work. You might convince one or more acquaintances to become licensed at the same time you do, or you might locate someone looking for a crew member when you take your written exam or attend rules meetings.

Contact the athletic director at area schools and colleges and the city recreation director or the recreation director at other places where athletic contests are held. Since sports officiators are usually booked in advance for the entire season, it is necessary to make your contacts well ahead of when the season starts. Once you have officiated a few contests and have done a satisfactory job, it will be easy to get contracts for the next year's season.

The pay for sports officiating varies with the type of sports activity, from state to state, and even from school to school within a state. As an example though, each officiator might expect to earn $30 to $50 for officiating a high school basketball double-header (junior varsity and varsity games) or $25 to $40 for a high school football game. The pay is generally lower for junior high games or those in a city recreation league or similar league. The pay is usually higher for junior college, four-year college and university, and tournament games.

Sports officiating can be a great way to keep alive an interest in athletics, to keep in shape, and to earn good extra money by working a few nights per week. For the person who comes to love sports officiating and who is good at it, potential exists for a full-time career as a professional sports officiator. This is a very difficult profession to enter, since the standards are high and people must work their way up through the minor leagues before they make it to the major leagues. For the select few who make it, though, the rewards are great, both financially and otherwise.

The person who truly enjoys and understands athletics might also earn extra money part time by becoming an *athletic scout*. In one application of this idea, you would scout opponent's teams for a high school or college and record data about their style of play, strengths, weaknesses, and so on. In another application, you would make contact with college or professional teams and identify and help land potential athletes in your geographic area for them.

You might also operate or assist with a *sports clinic* such as a basketball camp, baseball clinic, or football camp. The activities include lining up training facilities, lodging, and food services for a clinic lasting three days to a week. You might appeal to any age group, but junior high and high school students are usually the most receptive. Your function is to teach basic procedures of the game and to develop the participant's skills as well as to provide them with an enjoyable time. In order to attract participants, at least one of the clinic coaches should be a well-known and respected coach from the high school, college, or professional ranks or be a present or former college or professional player.

Storage Facility Operator

IT HAS been said that the way to earn more money than you can make through your own personal efforts is to put money to work for you or to put people to work for you. There's another possibility—put a *building* to work for you, as a *storage facility operator.*

A storage facility operator rents out storage space in a building, usually to more than one customer. Often, dozens of people or businesses will have goods stored in the facility.

Almost any type of commercial building, large garage, or outbuilding has potential. For most purposes, a hard-surface floor is necessary. The building may or may not be heated or air-conditioned, depending upon the type of goods accepted for storage. The building should be burglar-proof and fireproof.

The structure might be partitioned off into individual storage areas with an exterior door to each storage unit. In effect, this facility would look like and function like a series of single- or double-stall automobile garages. Customers have a key to their own units and can enter at any time they like, depositing and removing goods at will. This type of building arrangement provides a relatively work-free way to moonlight for the storage facility operator. About the only work involved is locating a new renter when a space becomes vacant, maintaining the building, and collecting rents.

A second type of structure is one that is not partitioned. The interior is wide open, and there are one or two doors to the building. The storage facility operator retains all keys to the doors, and a customer must contact the operator to gain entry to the building. This type of structure is not well suited to situations where customers will be depositing and removing goods frequently. It can be ideal, though, for storage of seasonal items, like boats, where all customers deliver the items in the fall and retrieve them in the spring.

Many situations exist for which people will rent space in a storage facility. These include storage of large seasonal articles like snowmobiles, boats, motorcycles, riding lawn mowers, and garden tractors. Automobiles and furniture are other personal property that are frequently stored. Businesses are also good customers for storage of inventory and unused fixtures. Usually, all you need do is run a few well-worded advertisements in local newspapers and you will be contacted by customers eager to use your storage facilities. You might also contact local businesses in person or via direct mail and inform real estate agents of your service, since they may be able to refer customers to you.

The agreement between you and the renter should be in writing and should set forth the duties and responsibilities of both parties. It should also state any types of products that are prohibited in the storage facility, like flammable liquids or explosives.

The agreement may be a *lease*, but it will be more advantageous to you if it is worded so that a *mutual benefit bailment* is established. The difference is in the wording of the agreement and in the amount of responsibility placed upon you for losses incurred by your customer because of theft or damage to the property. Under a mutual benefit bailment, you are required to give "ordinary care" for the goods. If they are damaged by third parties (someone other than you or your customer) or by acts of God (wind, lightning, etc.), you are not responsible.

If loss or damage to the property occurs because of your negligence in not properly maintaining or supervising the structure, you will be responsible regardless of whether the agreement is a lease or a mutual benefit bailment. You can obtain insurance to protect yourself against this potential loss.

If your agreement is a mutual benefit bailment, the term *renter* as used in this article is not technically correct. Your customer is called the *bailor* and you are called the *bailee*.

Have your attorney draw up a form contract that specifies

all the usual terms and provides blanks to fill in data like the date and rental amount, which vary from customer to customer.

If you have an existing building, you need only convert it to use as a storage facility. If not, you will need to buy or build one. This can amount to a substantial investment and you should carefully project expected income, costs, and expenses before proceeding, to determine if it appears to be a profitable venture. If you keep building or remodeling costs in line and manage the property efficiently to obtain maximum occupancy, it can provide steady, year-after-year profits.

Be certain that you check city or county *zoning ordinances* before you get too far along in your planning, to be certain that your structure can be used for your intended purpose.

Base your rental fee at a rate per square foot of floor space occupied or at a set amount for seasonal storage. This should be in line with that charged by other storage facilities in the area and with what customers are willing to pay. If your facilities offer a better location, easier accessibility, higher security, or other advantages, you can accordingly charge more than competitors.

Operating a storage facility can be one of the most carefree ways to moonlight. Once the structure is ready for use and all space has been rented, little attention is required. It is an excellent way to build up long-term equity by letting the rental fees pay all costs, expenses, and payments on the structure. The end result is that you will have a valuable building that is bought and paid for—by your customers.

Another area you might consider is operating a *rental service store*. Here, you would acquire items like garden tillers, extension ladders, cement mixers, punch bowls, and other items that people use infrequently and rent them out on an hourly, daily, or weekly basis.

Teacher

Do you know something—anything? If so, you can moonlight as a *teacher*. This is an ideal moonlighting activity for the millions of former and present classroom teachers, but it is by no means limited to those with professional training and certification.

Let us, however, explore the many opportunities for certified teachers first. There are many. These include teaching evening, weekend, summer, and off-campus courses for local public school systems, community colleges, business schools, vocational-technical schools, specialized institutes, and four-year colleges and universities. Since many of these educational institutions' regular staff members prefer not to teach these extra courses, administrators and coordinators must often seek qualified teachers from outside the system. This is where you come in. If you do not have the exact certification required, this can often be circumvented by obtaining temporary approval to teach on an occasional basis.

Many opportunities exist to be a teacher, even though you may not have teacher certification or any formal training at all. These include teaching noncredit adult courses through a public school system, community college, or vocational-technical institute in your area. Courses in woodworking, decoupage, welding, ceramics, bridge, gourmet cooking, computer operation, dancing, drawing, gardening, flower arranging, childbirth, photography, interior decorating, fencing, golf, or just about any topic imaginable are all possibilities.

If teaching for some type of educational institution appeals to you, contact school administrators, department chairpersons, or adult- and continuing-education coordinators to determine what opportunities might exist.

You can also offer your teaching services to business and industry, since many employers furnish educational programs for their employees. Many of these courses are academically oriented, but others are in recreational or personal-interest areas. Develop an idea for a course or seminar that you think (know) will be of value or interest to employees and approach the personnel department with your proposal. Most likely, your ambitious nature will be warmly received and your proposal will be given serious consideration.

In a related area, you may be able to teach seminars or short courses through *retail store education programs*. For example, if your expertise is in sewing, a fabric shop or sewing center will be delighted to pay you for offering a program for its customers, since it will increase sales of fabrics and sewing machines. Regardless of your specialty, be it ceramics, knitting, scuba diving, tennis, or insulation and weatherproofing techniques, there is probably some business that can use your services. All you have to do is ask.

Perhaps, instead of teaching for someone else, you would prefer to offer *private lessons*. Virtually anything that anyone has a desire to learn is a suitable topic. In the sports area, tennis, golf, snow skiing, water skiing, scuba diving, swimming, racquetball, and running are good possibilities. Games instruction, like bridge, backgammon, and chess, will be popular with many.

A vast market exists for *music lessons* in voice, piano, organ, guitar, or almost any other instrument. *Personal improvement classes* in weight loss, exercise, and aerobics are immensely popular. *Arts and crafts* is another large area with lessons in needlepoint, crocheting, leatherwork, quilting, jewelry making, candlemaking, and embroidery being just a few of the many possibilities.

The kitchen provides another interest area with gourmet cooking and cake decorating being worth consideration. Or lessons can be given in drawing, oil painting, photography, horseback riding, dancing, and many other areas.

Another possibility in the private-lessons area is *tutoring*, whereby you help students master a difficult subject area. Ele-

mentary, junior high, high school, and college students are potential users of this service.

Then too, you might operate a *pre-license school*. Here, you
would offer instruction for persons who must pass a state examination before they can become licensed to enter a profession
such as real estate, insurance, or cosmetology. You could offer
either a bona fide course covering perhaps 30 to 60 hours of
instruction or you could conduct concentrated one-, two-, or
three-day seminars, held just prior to the test date. In a related
area, you could conduct state-approved *recertification courses* for
those who need annual continuing education to renew their licenses.

When providing private lessons, either individual or group
instruction can be offered, depending upon the nature of what
you are teaching. Many of the courses can be taught in your
home, while others will require specialized facilities for which
arrangements must be made.

If you teach for a school system, business, or someone else,
your primary investment is your time. You will ordinarily not
need to buy equipment, materials, and supplies or spend time
or money in advertising and promotion.

If you offer private lessons, you may need to equip a classroom or studio in your home or in rented facilities. You will also
have full responsibility for all costs and activities involved in
promoting and advertising your offerings.

If you teach for someone else, you will be paid at an hourly
rate or a flat amount for the course. This rate can vary widely,
depending upon the type of employer and the nature of the
course. For example, though, earnings might be in the range of
two to four times the minimum wage rate for teaching a general-
interest course like knitting, exercise, or welding. Teaching a
highly technical course or one that is offered for college credit
might command earnings at five to ten times the minimum wage
rate.

If you offer your own private lessons, you should set your

enrollment fee at a charge per hour or at a flat amount for the course. The rate charged can vary greatly depending upon whether individual or group lessons are offered. You might charge in the range of three to five times the minimum wage rate per hour for private lessons. Your charge per student will most likely be lower for group lessons, but you can earn an outstanding hourly income if there are a large number of students in the group. You might also be able to supplement your income by selling supplies and materials to your students.

Besides the monetary payment, moonlighting as a teacher will provide you with the same intangible reward that attracts nearly all teachers to the field—the joy of helping others learn and the feeling of accomplishment that comes from watching their progress. Also, it is a great way to pursue your favorite area of interest and develop your own knowledge and skill in that area at the same time.

Another related moonlighting possibility, if you can organize a red-hot two- to eight-hour presentation in some area that is of great interest to many people, is to hit the speakers' circuit as a *seminar presenter*. Titles like "How to Stop Smoking," "How to Become a Millionaire," "How to Legally Avoid Paying Taxes," and "How to Earn Money at Home" may have great appeal. You must, of course, deliver what you promise or your seminar-presenting career will be short lived.

Income potential can be phenomenal if you truly are an expert in a popular topic and can conduct a worthwhile, exciting seminar that leaves the participants begging for more. Fees of several hundred dollars per presentation are not uncommon, and many popular speakers command many times that amount.

Towing Service

Here's a simple and easy moonlighting activity for the person who owns a pickup truck or wants to own one and have a way to pay for the truck at the same time. You can operate a *towing service*. Wait a minute! Don't you need a tow truck to operate a towing service? Well, yes and no. Yes, you need a tow truck, and no, you don't need one of those huge, cumbersome units you see at a salvage yard.

Let me explain. A product called Stow-n-tow is available and converts a pickup truck to a tow truck while still leaving the pickup in its basic condition for almost any normal use. The unit is contained in a heavy-duty metal "box" that covers the bed of the pickup. This box is only six inches high, and the tow unit is contained inside. When the tow unit is needed, a lever is pulled, the boom raises out of the box, and the towing harness is attached. Presto! In a minute or so, the pickup truck has been converted to a tow truck. You hook on the vehicle to be towed, and away you go. After use, the unit stows back in the box.

These units are available for full-size pickups with an eight-foot bed or for mini-size pickups with a six-foot bed. The larger unit can be used to tow any automobile, pickup truck, or van. The smaller unit's use is limited to mini-size automobiles and pickups.

The unit bolts to the pickup's frame without any modification required and without use of specialized tools or technical knowledge. A cable from the unit is connected to the pickup's battery. Installation time is only about an hour. A winch package is also available.

The cost of the unit is a fraction of what a full-scale tow truck costs, and about four to five average-priced tows per month will pay for it. For more information on the Stow-n-tow unit, contact an area distributor, or the manufacturer, Obbink Industries, Inc., 101 6th Street, Armstrong, IA 50514.

Besides acquiring the unit described above, other possibilities exist to become equipped to operate your towing service. These include buying a used tow truck or having a custom-built boom attached to your pickup or truck.

Once you have your tow truck ready to go, you are ready for your first customer. Advertise in the local newspaper and in the yellow pages of the telephone directory. This will bring many calls from persons whose cars have stalled or refuse to start. Also contact the police department, city Street Department, parking ramps, credit collection agencies, and others in the community who may have occasion to have vehicles towed away. Other good potential customers are gasoline service stations, small auto repair shops, and body shops who do not own a tow truck and therefore need to hire someone to do their towing. Even large, well-equipped towing services and garages might subcontract work to you during peak periods when there are more customers than they can handle with their own fleet.

Set your fee at a flat rate for local tows or at a flat rate plus a charge per mile. For long-distance tows, a flat rate plus a charge per mile is normal. Keep your rates in line with those charged by other towing services in the area. In fact, since your overhead and operating costs are low, you can charge lower rates, if you like, and still make an outstanding profit.

You might also equip your truck with jumper cables and a gas-powered battery charger. This will expand your services considerably so that you can first try to start vehicles with an apparently dead battery and then, if that doesn't work, you can tow the vehicle to a repair shop.

The primary investment in establishing a towing service is for your tow truck and for any other equipment you need for additional services offered. Beyond that, you need only a telephone available in your home for business calls. If you feel a business location is necessary, you will, of course, have additional rental and utilities charges.

Licensing or permit requirements vary from state to state

for operating a towing service. Check with your State Department of Commerce and also with the city clerk to determine if there are any local regulations. If a permit is required, the procedure is usually to complete an application and to submit a modest fee. Also, inform your insurance agent of the intended use of your vehicle, since extended coverage will be necessary.

How much can be earned operating a towing service? You can answer that question easily yourself by picking up the telephone and quizzing a few area towing services about their rates. Then, multiply the rate times the number of tows you expect per week or per month. This number is difficult to estimate, but it is not unusual for active towing services in a populated area to have dozens of customers per day and more than that in peak winter seasons. Even if you average only two or three tows per week, at perhaps a charge of $20 to $40 per tow, you will find that the income potential is outstanding.

If you have the time and ability, you can expand your services into other auto-related areas such as *auto tune-ups*, *auto repair*, or *body repair work*.

Trapper

IF THERE is a little bit of mountaineer in you, the most enjoyable and exciting way to moonlight may be as a *trapper*. Opportunities exist to follow this pursuit in virtually every state in the country, with muskrat, mink, fox, raccoon, and coyote being the main prey.

A trapper's activities are easy to describe. First, you set traps in areas inhabited by the type of animals you are stalking. Then, you check the traps daily. If you have caught your game, you will remove it and reset the trap, either in that same location or in a new one. If the trap is empty, you will either leave the trap where it is, after checking that everything is still set properly, or move it to a different location. You can either skin the animal and stretch and dry the pelt or freeze the entire carcass without skinning it out. You can usually sell your bounty to a fur buyer in either condition.

To be successful as a trapper, you will need to be familiar with the animals' habits and habitat. Much of this can be learned through reading, study, and inquiry of seasoned trappers. Experience, of course, is also extremely important, and you will become increasingly more successful as you develop a "feel" for where and how to set the traps.

Each state sets its own trapping season, which generally runs from late October or early November through the end of the year. Trapping season starts earlier in the West and ends later in the South. Some devoted (professional) trappers take advantage of this "shifting" season to follow the "trapping circuit" from one state to another in order to lengthen their annual trapping time.

Trappers are licensed in each state through the Fish and Game Division or Licensing Division of the Department of Natural Resources. Licenses can be obtained locally through the county recorder or, in some states, from sporting goods stores. An additional permit is needed in some states in order to trap on state-owned water or land. This is usually issued by the Conservation Commission and is available locally.

Licensing reciprocity exists between some neighboring states, which means that, if you are licensed in your home state, you can also trap in the neighboring state without obtaining an additional license there. Residents of the neighboring state can likewise trap in your state under the same arrangement. Where a reciprocity agreement is not in effect, some states gladly issue licenses to out-of-state trappers. Others refuse to do so to keep professional trappers out of the state.

Usually, there is no limit on the number of animals that can be captured. If, however, because of a severe winter or other reason, a species' ranks have been thinned out naturally, the state might shorten the season or otherwise restrict trapping.

The primary equipment you will need to become a trapper is a collection of animal traps. If you trap in more than one state, you must become familiar with each state's regulations, since some states require that certain types of traps be used. You will also need waders or hip boots, rubber gloves, a trapper's basket (like a backpack), and stakes to which the traps can be attached. If you skin your own animals, you will need several knives and stretching racks. A freezer will be needed to hold the carcasses if you do not do your own skinning. An investment of several hundred dollars will be necessary to get set up as a well-equipped, moderately serious trapper.

If you pursue trapping with extreme seriousness and dedication, you will also, in many areas of the country, need a boat, one or more motors, and other equipment to make your work faster and easier. Your total investment may run into several thousand dollars to become equipped in this fashion.

Since you probably already own some of the clothing and equipment that will be needed to become a trapper, your cash outlay will most likely be less than indicated here.

Your income as a trapper will vary with the number of traps you set, how hard you work at it, and the prices paid for pelts. These prices can swing widely, with prices being perhaps ten times as high in good years as they are in bad years. If you stick with trapping year after year, though, the prices will average out to a reasonable range. In an average year, if you set, say, 100 traps and work your line conscientiously, perhaps four hours per day, you can probably earn several thousand dollars in a 10-week trapping season. If you work at it extremely hard, by setting perhaps 300 traps and working at it eight hours per day, your income might hit five figures for an eight- to ten-week season. These projections are, of course, based upon there being fairly plentiful game and reasonable prices.

Because of the relatively short trapping season and the time of year, it is often the ideal moonlighting activity for those who work a seasonal job with a winter layoff, like road-construction workers in some parts of the country. It can also be ideal for persons who are self-employed and want a change of pace or for persons who want to turn their vacation time into an exciting money-maker.

Fur buyers usually pay higher prices if you have skinned, stretched, and dryed the pelts, since they do not need to do this work. They are often willing to buy unskinned animals, though, since they can sell the carcasses to a mink rancher or rendering company. If you have captured a large number of animals, you too can probably skin them and sell the carcasses. Prices paid can, and probably will, vary from one fur buyer to another. Therefore, you should shop around before selling your goods.

Besides trapping the type of animals described here, potential also exists to trap *turtles*. This is ordinarily not as profitable as trapping mink, muskrat, fox, and the others, but it provides a chance to keep active in trapping during the summer season. Ordinarily, a license is required. The turtles are sold to regular fur buyers to be resold for meat.

You might consider combining your interest in trapping with a knowledge of business to become a *fur buyer*. Here, you would buy pelts, unskinned animals, and even turtles from trappers. You would then sell them to another fur buyer, more advanced in the marketing chain than yourself. If you can accumulate a large number of pelts, you can then sell directly to brokers like the Hudson's Bay Company or Midwest Fur Company, both of which are located in New York.

Besides obtaining a state license, you need two primary qualifications to become a fur buyer: good contacts and lots of cash. The income potential is excellent, since a markup of 50 percent or more can often be obtained on furs when they are sold. This too, like trapping, is seasonal, with a two- to three-month active work season.

Typewriting Service

ALL THE ads you see in newspapers and tabloids are right—you *can* earn money by operating a *typewriting service*. The problem is that virtually no one running such an advertisement is going to hand you a job as a typist—or a job addressing or stuffing envelopes, for that matter. You must develop your own business and locate your own clientele—neither of which is difficult to do.

First, you must possess well-developed typing skills. Since you will probably charge by the page typed rather than by the hour, your typing must be fast and accurate in order for you to earn a suitable rate of pay. You will need to be familiar with various letter styles and manuscript styles and must be able to read and follow style manuals and directions furnished to you by your customers. A knowledge of various grades and qualities of paper, typewriter ribbons, and error-correcting materials is also necessary. In addition, you will need to make undetectable corrections of typographical errors.

Since some of your customers' grammar skills will be less developed than they should be (horrible, actually), you will need to have a good command in this area so that you can straighten out glaring errors as you go.

The primary equipment you will need includes a good typewriter that uses a film ribbon and produces a high-quality finished product, typewriter ribbons, error-correcting materials, and a few reference books. At a minimum, a suitable typewriter will cost several hundred dollars, and you may easily spend well over a thousand dollars to obtain the professional model you want. Usually, the more expensive machines can be acquired on a lease-purchase arrangement or installment purchase basis whereby monthly payments are made. Therefore, you can pay for the typewriter from your earnings. If you intend to seriously offer your typewriting service for many years to come, you might consider purchasing word processing equipment, which can speed up your production rate considerably.

For large jobs, you should usually require your clients to furnish their own paper so they get the grade and quality they want and so that you do not need to be bothered with the task of purchasing it. For small jobs, it will probably be easier for you to furnish the paper and include its cost in your fee.

Clients for your service can be found almost anywhere. If you live in a college or university town, student term papers, master's theses, and doctoral dissertations will keep you very busy. Just advertise in the college newspaper and post notices on campus and dormitory bulletin boards.

Businesses are another category of clients. Often, insurance agencies, real estate offices, financial institutions, accountants, and others have a special mailing that requires individually typed letters or envelopes and that is too voluminous for their regular staff to handle. Hiring you makes good sense, since you can do the work at your own office or home without interfering with the business's normal operation. One technique you can use to land business accounts is to send them a letter, perfectly typed, of course, describing your service.

Individuals needing professionally typed materials for dozens of different purposes are also good clients. These might include a would-be author with a full-length manuscript, a job applicant needing to send a professional-looking application letter or resumé, or someone needing to send a high-quality personal business letter to a company.

Ordinarily, typists charge by the page. The rate will vary depending upon whether the material is to be single- or double-spaced or if carbon copies are to be produced. The condition of the client's rough draft will also affect the price you charge. If it is sloppily handwritten or needs an unusual amount of grammatical, spelling, or punctuation corrections, the rate will be understandably higher. The nature of the copy will also affect your rate, since highly technical or scientific data may take far longer to type than standard copy. All in all, typists ordinarily earn from two to four times the minimum wage rate per hour, depending upon their own level of typing speed, accuracy, and efficiency.

Operating a typewriting service can be an ideal way to moonlight in that you can most likely do all your work right at home if you wish. Individuals will deliver their rough drafts to you and pick up the finished products. Business clients, however, will probably require that you do all the legwork.

Usually, you will have a deadline for each project that is several days, weeks, or months in the future. This, and the fact that you can work at the typing whenever you have a spare hour or so, allows you great flexibility in your day-to-day time schedule.

If you land more jobs than you can personally handle, you can easily enlarge your typewriting service, and income, by hiring other highly qualified and conscientious typists to help you. You will pay them less per page than you receive from your clients, thus making an additional profit.

You might also expand into other related areas like offering a full-fledged *mail processing service* for businesses, whereby you address envelopes, and type, fold, and insert materials for mailing.

Vacuum Cleaner Sales

How would you like to sell a product that is used in virtually every household in the country? It is handy to transport, easy to operate, ideal for demonstrations, and you can make a high commission on each sale. Well, that is the very nature of *vacuum cleaner sales*. Stop. Don't turn the page before you read the rest of this article; selling vacuum cleaners may be far more interesting, appealing, and profitable than you realize.

The sales-organization structure varies somewhat from one vacuum cleaner company to another, but, in most regards, they are very similar. Someone starting as a vacuum cleaner salesperson would initially begin as a *dealer* or *assistant dealer*. The main difference here is that a dealer can usually have assistant dealers work under him, whereas the assistant dealer cannot. The dealer receives a small override on all sales made by the assistant dealer. Other than that, they perform about the same activities. In effect, dealers and assistant dealers perform a role similar to that of retail stores—they sell the product directly to the ultimate user.

Dealers or assistant dealers usually receive their vacuum cleaners from a *distributor*. The distributor is a wholesaler, who receives the vacuum cleaners directly from the factory.

Usually, after making a certain number of sales, an assistant dealer can become a dealer. Likewise, a dealer who shows substantial sales over an extended period may be able to become a distributor.

Some companies give exclusive territories or franchised areas to their salespeople while other companies allow dealers to sell wherever they want.

A dealer or assistant dealer can operate from a business location or from home. Some sales are made to walk-in customers, but traditionally, vacuum cleaners are *sold* rather than *bought*. This means that the vacuum cleaner salesperson must ordinarily prospect for customers and demonstrate the unit at the prospect's home or business.

Prospecting is one of the keys to success in vacuum cleaner sales.

Many names of prospects can be gathered through a referral technique by asking present customers and prospects if they know of someone else who could use a new vacuum cleaner. The newspaper is a good source of prospects. Engagement announcements identify those who will soon be setting up house-keeping and who therefore will need a vacuum cleaner, one of yours.

Many names can also be gathered by manning a demonstration booth at a county fair, home show, or similar event that draws large numbers of people. You might also use *cold calls*, going door to door or calling names at random from the telephone directory.

After you have identified a prospect who has an interest in a vacuum cleaner, you must make a sales presentation. Often, this takes place at the prospect's home or business by appointment. The most powerful part of your presentation is the demonstration, where you show what your cleaner will do.

Closing the sale is the final, and often most difficult, step. A knowledge of trade-in arrangements and financing methods will be necessary tools.

Your earnings from a single sale can be outstanding. The amounts and procedures vary from company to company, but the following may be indicative of what to expect. Let's assume that the manufacturer's suggested retail price for the vacuum cleaner, plus attachments, is $600. The price you must pay your distributor for it is $400. Therefore, if you sell it at the suggested price, you will earn $200. Often, however, customers haggle on price, and you might end up selling at $550—still a handsome $150 profit. If you cut prices too low, your company may become upset, and just as bad, you make very little profit for your efforts.

Some vacuum cleaner companies require that their dealers and assistant dealers buy their cleaners outright, paying for them within a certain time after delivery. With other companies, the machines are placed with you on consignment, meaning that you do not pay for them until they are sold.

Your investment in entering vacuum cleaner sales is usually low, since you can probably receive your initial machine on consignment or have a reasonable time within which you can pay for it. Other costs will vary, depending upon your business location and method of operation. You can probably get started in business for less than a hundred dollars, which might include some initial advertising on your part.

Selling vacuum cleaners may be the ideal moonlighting activity for the person who likes direct sales to consumers. You can set your own hours and work by appointment only. The potential also exists to build a sales organization with several assistant dealers beneath you and, after that, to become a distributor with many dealers in your territory.

Additional money can be made by selling supplies such as drive belts and dust bags. If the company allows, you can also repair machines for a service fee.

Prominent vacuum cleaner manufacturers, which you may wish to contact for specific information, are as follows: Electrolux, 2777 Summer Street, Stamford, CT 06905; Filter Queen, Health-Mor, Inc., 35-T East Wacker Drive, Chicago, IL 60601; Kirby Company, Division of Scott & Fetzer, 1920 West 114th Street, Cleveland, OH 44102.

A related area you might consider is *sewing machine sales*. You would sell for a local sewing machine retailer rather than a manufacturer, but the potential income per sale would still be high. If this sounds interesting, contact any local sewing machine center—they will be delighted to discuss this proposition with you.

Vending Machine Route Operator

Here's your chance to get in on the hottest game in town—by moonlighting as a *vending machine route operator*.

As a vending machine route operator, you will buy or lease one or more types of coin-operated machines and place them in locations where customers will use them. Many types of machines are available that vend useful products or provide amusement and entertainment. These include pool tables, jukeboxes, electronic video games, pinball machines, foosball tables, and machines that vend sandwiches, beverages, cigarettes, candy, novelties, peanuts, and miscellaneous personal items. Coin-operated laundry equipment for installation in apartment buildings and dormitories is another possibility.

There are two principal ingredients for success in operating a vending machine route. Foremost of these is securing good locations for your machines, where they will receive a high amount of "play." Since there is stiff competition between vending machine route operators who are all seeking to land the prime locations, you will need to prospect well, get there first, and make your offerings and arrangements attractive.

Second, you must install the right equipment to deliver the type of product, service, or entertainment that customers want. What constitutes the "right" equipment can change quickly in the vending business, particularly in the amusement area. At any one time, there is probably one type of game or machine that is "hot" and will remain so for perhaps six months to two years, until it is replaced by the newest fad. Getting in on the new fad early can pay big dividends. If you guess wrong, however, you may be stuck with machines that attract little attention. Some types of amusement machines, like jukeboxes and pool tables, have enjoyed a steady and proven popularity that has not waned through the years. Food and beverage machines in industrial or college locations and coin-operated laundry equipment can also provide steady income year in and year out.

Vending equipment can be purchased outright or secured on a lease-purchase arrangement from distributors. Usually, the lease-purchase programs are short term, perhaps calling for full payment in one or two years. This results in rather high monthly payments. Therefore, many vending machine route operators prefer to pay cash or to arrange for an installment loan through their local bank. Ordinarily, repayment can be made over two to three years with relatively low monthly payments.

Vending machines are secured from distributors, who can be located by checking the yellow pages of a city telephone directory. Ordinarily, manufacturers do not sell directly to vending machine route operators.

Usually, the vending machine route operator and the owner of the business where the machine is placed share in the income generated by the machine. They may use a 50-50 split or any other division agreed to by the parties. How active the location is generally determines what split will be satisfactory to you, since you must receive enough income to provide a return on your investment, to pay you for your time, and to cover your risk.

If the location is relatively inactive, you may need 60 percent or more of the total income to make it worth your while to place a machine at that site. If the location is extremely slow, you might take all the proceeds and even charge the business owner an additional fee for the convenience of having the machine on the premises. Under another arrangement, you might lease the machine to a business for a flat amount per month and allow the business to retain all income from the machine.

The amount of time required to service your route will vary with the type of machines you operate. Food and beverage vending machines may need daily refilling, while games and jukeboxes may need to be checked but once a week or once a month, and then only to empty the coin container.

Each state has its own licensing requirements pertaining to vending machines. Ordinarily, each machine must be licensed through some department, perhaps the State Department of Agriculture. Many cities and counties also require their own license or permit. In addition, if you vend food or cigarettes, a permit or license will be needed from the State Department of Agriculture and/or local officials.

If you use recorded music for profit, as with a jukebox or background-music system, you may need to pay performance royalties similar to those paid by radio stations, nightclubs, and others. The licensing agencies that collect these fees for the benefit of composers, musicians, and publishers are Broadcast Music, Inc. (BMI) and American Society of Composers and Publishers (ASCAP). Most likely, a representative from one of these organizations will contact you if they require payment.

Equipment needed to establish your vending machine route includes a truck or van to transport your machines, a cart or dolly, and a few miscellaneous hand tools. Your primary investment will be for the vending machines and amusement games, which may easily cost several thousand dollars each. Perhaps this seems high, but an average vending machine can probably pay for itself within three years. A "hot" machine in a prime location may be able to accomplish this feat in six months or less. After that, the income generated is nearly clear profit. Once it is paid for, an average machine may yield over a thousand dollars of profit per year. A popular machine in a prime location may generate several times that amount.

Vending machines and amusement games will earn you no profit unless they are on the job and are in tip-top operating condition. Therefore, you must either be able to repair them yourself or must have a reliable repair shop available that will give service on short notice.

General mechanical knowledge and common sense may be sufficient to repair some of the more basic mechanical vending machines. The electronic machines and games are another story, however. Knowledge of electronics is necessary and training of perhaps two or three days on specific machines may be required. Many manufacturers sponsor two- or three-week training sessions at their home offices or offer two- or three-day schools at their distributors' locations. These are ideal for the person who already has a command of basic electronics.

This discussion reveals another moonlighting opportunity—*repairing and servicing* vending machines and amusement games. Since this is a specialized area, you can command a handsome hourly wage that is perhaps four to six times the minimum wage rate. This can be ideal for the person who has knowledge or interest in the electronics area.

Other opportunities can exist as an *assistant* to a vending machine route operator. Here, you would help install and remove equipment, make periodic rounds to check the equipment's condition, or restock machines with food, beverages, and other products.

Still another possibility is to operate an *arcade* that is jammed with pinball machines, pool tables, electronic video games, and other machines for entertainment and amusement. If you already operate a vending machine route, this can be a natural extension of your activities and a way to ensure that you will never have a machine sitting idle.

If you do not own any entertainment, amusement, or vending machines, you can still operate an arcade by having the vending machine operator install the equipment on a percentage basis at no investment cost to you.

Welcoming Service

IF YOU meet people easily, enjoy making new friends, and feel good when you do something nice for someone, you might consider operating a *welcoming service* as your method of moonlighting.

Everyone probably has the same general image of what activities are performed by someone operating a welcoming service. That is, greeting newcomers to the community and providing them with a number of free gifts and coupons that can be redeemed at local businesses. This is only the most visible part of the job, however.

In reality, a welcoming service is actually an *advertising service*, operated to inform newcomers about each participating merchant's goods and services and designed to attract them to the merchant's place of business as a customer. Here's how it works. You contact local merchants and convince them to provide you with small gifts and/or redeemable coupons that will be delivered to newcomers in your community at no charge to the recipient. You then personally deliver these gifts and coupons, which in reality are advertisements, to the newcomers. For doing so, each merchant will pay a certain fee for each newcomer you contact. You will regularly provide each merchant with a list of newcomers you have contacted and to whom you have delivered the advertising materials. You will bill the merchant accordingly.

In addition to your clients' advertisements, you should include as many useful articles as possible in your packet of materials to make it more appealing and worthwhile. This might include a welcoming letter from the mayor, a brief history of the community, a map of the city, and lists of community services, schools, churches, recreational facilities, community organizations, and anything else that would be nice to know. Most of these materials will be gladly furnished free by the chamber of commerce or community-minded organizations.

The first step in operating a successful welcoming service is to develop a sizable clientele of merchants who will pay you for delivering their advertisements. You might set some self-imposed regulations, like representing only one business of each type in highly competitive areas, to make your offerings more attractive. You should also require the merchants to furnish their own advertising copy in a size and format that adheres to your guidelines. Perhaps you could require that all printing be done by a specific printer to ensure uniformity.

Charge each merchant a set fee, like two, three, or five dollars for each newcomer you contact. You may want to develop a rate schedule where businesses of different sizes and categories are charged varying fees.

Since your earnings are largely determined by the number

of newcomers you contact, prospecting for new arrivals in your community is a big part of your job. It is important that others in your community believe that you are providing a useful service, since you will be asking them to volunteer names of newcomers with whom they come in contact. Generally speaking, you should emphasize the service you are providing to the newcomers, and therefore to the community's image, and soft-peddle the fact that you are really an advertising salesperson.

On a regular basis, you should check with those people, businesses, and organizations that ordinarily come in contact with a person when they first move into the community. This includes real estate agencies, insurance offices, churches, utility companies, personnel managers of major industries, and elementary, junior high, and high school officials. You should also list your name under "Welcoming Services" in the telephone directory yellow pages and should occasionally run an advertisement in your local newspaper.

Even though your welcoming service is a bona fide business, many will look upon it as being a community service. Therefore, it is possible that you might even be listed free of charge in a chamber of commerce directory or might receive free advertising from the local media along with other community-oriented and public-information announcements.

Often, newcomers to your community will be eager to meet you and to receive the free gifts and coupons, so they will call you themselves to let you know that they have arrived. In fact, your advertisements should ask them to do so, and you should also encourage others in the community who come in contact with new arrivals to call you as well.

Your call on each newcomer will amount to more than just saying hello, dropping off the packet of materials, and leaving. You should thoroughly go through all of the materials with the newcomer and describe each participating business and their offerings in detail. Remember, you are an ambassador of the merchants who are paying you, and your job is to promote and advertise those businesses. Obviously, if only a few, or none, of the newcomers visit your participating merchants, they will soon decide that your service is ineffective, not worth the money, and they will drop it. On the other hand, if you deliver a large number of the community's new residents to your clients' doorsteps, they will stay with your service forever. Each visit to a newcomer, therefore, may easily last an hour or more.

At the end of each week or month, you will file a report with each merchant, giving them the name, address, phone number, and perhaps some personal data about each newcomer you have contacted. This is used in calculating your fee and also provides merchants with data for use in their own promotional programs.

Since you are primarily providing a service, the equipment you will need is limited to having a vehicle and a telephone available for business use. Operating costs are few, being confined mostly to advertising and vehicle expense. You may also wish to hire an answering service, since you would otherwise most likely miss many calls while you are out making your rounds.

Your earnings will depend upon the number of merchants you land as customers, the rates you charge them, and the number of contacts you make with newcomers. As an example, though, if you have 50 merchants as clients, who are each charged $2 for every contact you make, and if you contact 10 newcomers in a month, your gross earnings for the month would be $1,000 (50 × $2 × 10 = $1,000). Obviously, adding a few more merchants, charging higher rates, or making more contacts would substantially increase your earnings.

You can either establish and operate your own welcoming service or you can become affiliated with a regionally or nationally known welcoming-service company. The advantage of operating your own independent service is that you can organize it and operate it exactly as you wish. The disadvantage is that your operation will lack the prestige and recognition of a well-known name and most likely it will be more difficult to gain community support. Then too, a large and well-organized welcoming service company can offer you training, advice, and assistance, which should be very beneficial.

In addition to, or instead of, operating a welcoming service, several similar offerings hold good moneymaking potential for the moonlighter. A *recent parents congratulatory service* would provide advertisements from merchants who offer products for new parents and babies. A *recently engaged congratulatory service* provides information on products and businesses that will appeal to those who are soon to be married. Another possibility is to operate an *advertising delivery system*, where a select number of merchants' advertisements, say 10 to 15, are hand-delivered in a plastic sack to every resident in the community on a weekly basis. All three of these services operate on the same basic principles and along the same guidelines as a welcoming service.

Window Designer

NEXT TIME you're walking through the retail business district in your community, observe the displays in the store windows. Could you do better? If so, a fun moonlighting opportunity awaits you as a *window designer*.

As a window designer, you will design and decorate store windows. Your goal should be to produce displays that are attractive and attention-getting and which produce one ultimate result—they lure customers into the store. Since window displays are considered to be a form of advertising, it is their pulling power that is the ultimate measuring stick of your success. That point must always be kept firmly in mind.

If you know your business, your prospective clients will be easy to spot. They're the ones with lackluster, drab, ineffective window displays.

Before you approach a business manager, have an idea of

improvements you could offer. You should have a general theme in mind, or you might even develop a sketch to show what one of your displays would look like. As part of your proposal, you may need to educate the business owner or manager on the importance and value of a customer-drawing window display. This fact appears obvious, but sometimes the most obvious business principles are overlooked in the frantic day-to-day life of a retailer. You should also have a recommendation in mind for frequency of changing the displays, cost per display, and fee you will charge.

At first, a business manager may be reluctant to hire a window designer because of the seemingly additional labor cost. When you point out, however, that someone is currently being paid to prepare window displays, a regular employee, probably, and that you can do it more efficiently because you specialize in that area, this objection should be overcome. In addition, your providing this service will allow the regular employees to concentrate on their primary duties—selling the merchandise.

No special training is required to become a window designer, although several skills are necessary. Foremost among these is creativity. You must continually develop fresh ideas that attract attention and pack pulling power. A knowledge of color schemes, fabrics, building materials, and lighting is necessary. Also, you will need to have a basic understanding of your client's business philosophy so you can reflect that mood in your displays.

Being a window designer can be the perfect moonlighting activity for persons with ability in art, interior decoration, or advertising. Since two different aspects are involved in preparing window displays—creating them and building them—it might be an ideal activity for two persons with complementary skills.

You can provide your services for one large retailer only or you might prefer to handle several smaller clients. If you have several clients, you should avoid working for competing businesses, since doing so will tend to cancel out the competitive edge that you are trying to provide for your client.

Since you are primarily offering a service, little investment is required to become a window designer. You will need a few specialized tools, but your clients should be expected to pay for all materials and supplies that are necessary to construct the display.

Set your fee at a specific rate per window display, which is based upon providing you with a generous hourly income. Since yours is a specialized skill that eludes many people, you are entitled to be well paid, perhaps at three to five times the minimum wage rate per hour. You can easily control the amount of time you devote to this moonlighting activity, and your overall income, by the number of clients you accept.

Another possibility for your talent as a designer is in the field of *layout design*. Here, you would design an attractive and efficient layout for store fixtures, restaurant equipment, office furnishings, and so on.

Woodworking

ONE OF the all-time favorite hobbies, *woodworking*, also happens to be one of the all-time favorite ways to moonlight. Part of this is because it is so enjoyable and the other part is that it can be very profitable.

Perhaps you'll readily agree with the first part—that woodworking would be an enjoyable way to moonlight. The second part, though, may raise an eyebrow or two. Just what is it that a woodworker can build or make that would be profitable? Well, let's look at some possibilities.

Picture frames can be ideal for the person who wants something that is fairly easy to make and for which several potential markets exist. Interior decorators, furniture dealers, photographers, art galleries, limited-edition art reproduction dealers, artists, and individuals are all good contacts. Some of these will buy from you directly, while others will be happy to refer customers to you.

Wood toys are another favorite. Here, perhaps even more so than with most other homemade wood products, your finished goods will meet a great deal of competition in the marketplace. Not only will potential buyers compare them with other wood toys, but they must also stand up well against metal, plastic, fiber glass, and fabric toys. Likewise, they must withstand the assault of bells, whistles, buzzers, lights, and all sorts of gizmos attached to toys to attract a child's attention. Fear not, however, there is a market for wood toys, and if your trucks, cars, animals, or trains are high quality, many parents will buy them as a toy their child can enjoy and which, years later, is a valued keepsake.

Furniture is another good possibility. You can specialize in home desks, rocking chairs, and bookcases, or you might build children's products, such as table and chair sets, cradles, beds, and the like.

Other items worth considering include dollhouses, miniatures, picnic tables, bookends, lamps, and wall hangings. You might even specialize in the unusual, like wooden shoes or novelty items. On the other hand, you may prefer sticking to tried and proven projects like cabinetmaking or building storage sheds.

The actual woodworking is only half your job; the other part is marketing what you produce. In some cases, this may be fairly easy, while in others it will take time and effort to locate or develop distribution channels.

If you produce only a few items, you may be able to easily sell them yourself from your home or from your own retail location. In other cases, for instance if you are a cabinetmaker, you may be able to build on special order only.

If you produce a large number of items, you may not be able to sell them all yourself and will then need to rely on retailers or wholesalers. The first step in locating retailers to handle your goods is to identify the types of merchants who stock similar products. You might first attempt to sell them your goods outright, and if that fails, you might consider placing your goods in the store on consignment.

Under the consignment arrangement, the store does not pay you anything until they sell the goods. Since this is a rather risk-free way for retailers to stock your goods, they may be much more receptive to this plan at first than to buying your goods outright. The advantage of this arrangement to you is that it increases the chances of finding retailers who will stock your merchandise. The disadvantage is that you may have a large investment tied up for a long time while you wait for the goods to move off the retailers' shelves.

You can start small, with a few retailers, and if the goods sell well, you can increase the number of outlets, seek bigger stores, contract with chain operations, and perhaps try to locate wholesalers to distribute your goods in a wide area.

If you sell the finished product directly to the ultimate consumer, your prices must be in line with those charged by others for similar goods. If you sell to retailers, your prices need to be set so that the retailer can sell the items at competitive prices and make a normal profit at the same time. As a general rule, you should attempt to sell your products at twice their cost when selling to wholesalers.

The amount of investment required to establish your woodworking business will vary with the type of products you build. In all likelihood, you probably already have much of what you will need. Even if you must buy additional equipment, it will be something that you can use for your personal pleasure as well as for your part-time woodworking business.

As far as income potential is concerned, there are no guarantees. Conceivably, you might sell very few of your products; or, on the other hand, you might sell fabulous quantities. Most likely, your results will fall somewhere in between, which should provide a nice addition to your regular income. Certainly, the potential exists to develop your woodworking business into a thriving operation that produces a broad range of products that are widely distributed.

Related areas that provide ideal moonlighting activities include *furniture repair, antique repair, furniture refinishing,* and *antique refinishing.* If you enter the repair business, you may need to build authentic replacement parts for those pieces that are broken or missing and will need to glue, nail, and otherwise make sturdy any furniture that is wobbly or that has come apart altogether. If you enter the refinishing business, you will most likely need to become an expert on paint and stain removers and on various types of stains and finishes.

Any of these areas can be easily operated by themselves, in conjunction with each other, or with your woodworking activities.

Writing

THE AUTHOR would not feel *Moonlighting* complete unless his personal favorite was included—*writing.* This moonlighting activity is not for everyone, to be sure, but for the right person, it can be ideal.

Perhaps the mention of *writing* conjures up thoughts of someone sitting at a typewriter laboriously banging out a full-length novel. Yes, that is one avenue for your writing skills, but there are many other possibilities as well.

Let's look at writing the novel or other type of book first. It is probably accurate to say that getting a book published by a well-known publisher often fits in the "long-shot" category. This is because the competition is stiff and editors are overrun with a tremendous number of manuscripts from which they can select the cream of the crop for publication. This type of talk is not intended to dampen your enthusiasm, but rather, it is presented to give an accurate picture of the possibilities for success.

It is possible, however, to become a published author. This book, which you are now holding in your hands, is proof of that. In fact, some 40,000 books are published annually.

You can approach your book in one of two basic ways. One is to write the entire manuscript first and then set about finding a publisher. The other is to develop a comprehensive outline and a sample chapter or two for submission. Each method has its own advantages and disadvantages, and the amount of time you are willing to invest, with no guarantees of publication, might be your guide.

Book authors receive a royalty on all sales of the work. This consists of a percentage of the publisher's net receipts, usually in the 7 to 15 percent range, depending on the type of book and the author's previous writing success. Often, a cash advance against royalties is paid, with half being received when the contract is signed and the other half being received when the work is published.

Magazines are another possibility to consider for your writing efforts. Whatever area of knowledge or interest you possess— be it cooking, pets, sports, business, child care, arts and crafts, or anything else—you can rely on one thing: some magazine publishes articles in that area.

All magazines have a definite format and are designed with a specific topic or reader interest in mind. Therefore, it is necessary to become thoroughly familiar with each magazine's interests and needs before submitting an article for review. You should also study the length, general tone, and style of each magazine's articles and formulate your writing to fit that mold.

Payment arrangements for magazine articles include a per word rate or a flat amount per article. The total amount may range from less than a hundred dollars to several thousand dollars, depending upon the publication, the article's length, and other factors.

Most book and magazine publishers require that you send a letter of inquiry describing your proposal before submitting the manuscript. This procedure saves both you and the publisher a great deal of time, effort, and money.

Many publishers prefer to deal with literary agents rather than directly with writers. Therefore, you might attempt to secure an agent instead of making contacts with publishers. Follow the same process of manuscript preparation and send a letter of inquiry as described above. If an agent finds your work promising, he or she will then attempt to place it with a suitable publisher. For this service, the agent will charge a fee of perhaps 10 percent of whatever is earned on the sale.

Literary Market Place, which is available at most public and college libraries, is an excellent source of names and addresses of agents, publishers, and others in the publishing business.

Writing newspaper articles is another avenue to consider. One way to approach this is as a free-lance writer, whereby you write special-interest articles and sell them to an appropriate newspaper. Another approach is to contact a newspaper with an idea for a regular column on some topic in which many people in the community may have an interest. Ways to save money, child care, investment forecasts, and gardening are examples of topics that might be possibilities. You might write a "gossip" column or perhaps do entertainment reviews or even reviews of special events.

As a free-lance writer, you will be paid a flat amount per article used. As a regular feature writer, you will be paid a monthly salary or receive a certain amount per column.

The most important aspects of writing a book, magazine article, or newspaper article are the *idea* and the *approach*. If you have a unique, fresh, original idea, chances of gaining an editor's attention are greatly improved. Likewise, if you have a more unusual, and better, approach to a topic than others have used, your chances are increased. Ideally, you should have an original idea *and* an attractive approach in your method of presentation.

If you have specialized knowledge in some subject, you have a good indication of what your book or article should be about: write about that topic. If you have an interest in a topic but don't have the specialized knowledge, research until you learn the subject thoroughly.

Prepare your manuscript to be as professional looking as possible. Use a high-quality bond paper, utilize a typewriter with a good, dark ribbon, and make neat corrections of errors. Review and revise your manuscript until it is free of grammatical errors and is letter perfect in every regard.

After your first book or article is published, you will find that the publishers' doors will open much more easily for you. It will then be possible to produce a string of books or articles that can bring a steady and substantial income.

Another possibility to utilize your writing skills includes offering a *job résumé and letter-of-application service.* Since most people prepare résumés and letters of application for jobs infrequently, they are unfamiliar with how to prepare attention-getting ones that work. You can help organize their materials and might even provide a typing service where you prepare professionally typed papers for their use.

One of the major advantages that writing offers for a part-time career is flexibility. You have no set schedule to follow, except for deadlines, and can arrange each day's or week's writing to dovetail with your other activities. Another advantage is that you have very little cash investment in equipment and supplies; your main investment is time.

Whatever application you make of your writing skills, and regardless of the money you earn, the sheer feeling of accomplishment that comes from creating an original work is still one of the best rewards.

Miscellaneous Ideas

FIND the ideal way to moonlight in those previously described? If not, there's still hope! Perhaps one of the ideas briefly described below will be just what you are looking for.

Archery Range: There are probably more archery enthusiasts in your area than you realize. Even if there aren't, you can most likely stimulate enough interest to make operating an archery range a successful venture.

You can operate an indoor range, an outdoor range, or both. For an indoor target-shooting range, you should provide a shooting area that is 30 yards long. For an outdoor bow-hunting range, it is ideal to have a 50-yard distance available. Little equipment is required besides targets.

You can set your rates by the hour, or you might sell annual memberships. Income can be increased by establishing leagues and sponsoring tournaments. You may also wish to sell archery equipment, from which you will earn an extra profit and also increase avid archers' interest in the sport.

Aerial Photo Sales: This one is just what it sounds like—you take aerial photos of farms, ranches, and acreages and sell them to the property owner. If you are a pilot, photographer, or salesperson, you can team up with someone who possesses the other necessary skills and you're in business.

You might take photographs of every residence in a section or township, develop them, and set about contacting each resident individually. You can offer several sizes at varying prices. Extra money can be earned by selling frames for the photographs as well.

Assembler: If you have a modest amount of mechanical ability and like to work with your hands, you might moonlight as an assembler. Here, you would assemble products like bicycles, lawn mowers, snowblowers, garden tillers, or other similar products that are shipped to retailers in an unassembled state. Since the retail employees are often too busy to assemble these items or lack interest or ability for doing so, part-time assemblers are often hired.

The pay rate is usually at a set amount per item assembled, and you should be able to earn at about twice the minium wage rate once you become proficient.

Bail Bond Agent: You've heard of bail bond agents, but just what does one do? Well, a bail bond agent actually represents an insurance company that insures that someone who is released from jail will not abscond. If the person does flee, the insurance company pays a certain sum of money, the bond, which was set by the court.

The bonding agent writes the insurance policy for the person confined to jail, for which a substantial premium is charged, usually 10 percent of the bond that is posted. Therefore, if a $5,000 bond is required, the premium would be $500, which is shared by the insurance company and the bonding agent.

To become a bonding agent, it is usually necessary to pass an exam administered by the State Insurance Department. It should be mentioned that not all states use the services of bail bond agents.

Balloon Bouquet Sales: Because many people tire of the same old thing—flowers for Valentine's day, flowers for birthdays, flowers for anniversaries, flowers for Easter, flowers, flowers, flowers—you can offer an interesting change of pace by selling balloon bouquets.

A balloon bouquet is just what it sounds like—a bouquet made of helium-filled balloons. Special touches can be added with all sorts of ribbons, bows, printing on balloons, and whatever your imagination can produce.

You would advertise your service and make deliveries, just like a floral shop.

Contract Negotiator: State and federal collective bargaining laws require that a negotiation process for determining wages, fringe benefits, hours, and other work-related factors be available to many employers and employees. Many of those who become involved in such negotiations are relatively small in size, like school systems, hospitals, and local businesses. Often, neither the employer nor any of the employees is interested in handling negotiations or feels incompetent to do so. Therefore, they hire someone to negotiate their contract terms for them.

A background in labor relations, contracts, speech, sales, or debate will be very helpful in entering this interesting field. Perhaps the easiest way to gain your training is to become involved in contract negotiations at your current place of employment. You can then branch out to offer your services to others.

Since this is a specialized area, contract negotiators often receive an outstanding rate of pay, which might amount to 5 to 10 times the minimum wage rate per hour or several hundred dollars for a full-day session.

Coupon Refunding: Here's a way to make money by saving money. Dedicate a few hours per week to clipping coupons from magazines and newspapers, to collecting proof-of-purchase labels, and to sorting, organizing, and filing them. Then, when you go on your weekly grocery and household-item shopping trip, use the coupons and labels to get discounts on items you buy. Also, look for coupons or discounts on product packages and be alert for manufacturers' rebates in the form of cash or products.

It will take a little while to develop the knack for coupon refunding, but once you do, you will be able to save a substantial portion of the cost of your bill for food and household items, perhaps as much as 30 to 50 percent or more of your current expenditures.

Driving Range: If you have a strip of ground that is 450 yards or so long, you might consider establishing a driving range where golfers can practice their swings. The ground should be covered with nicely mowed grass similar to that found on a golf course, and markers should indicate various distances.

Charge a fee for each bucket of golf balls checked out by a customer.

Judging: Are you an expert in some topic that would entitle you to become a judge at contests, county fairs, and similar events? If so, you can have a great deal of fun, bask in the limelight, increase your prestige among your colleagues, and earn some extra money all at the same time.

Notary Public: Some people might assume that such an official-sounding title as notary public is difficult to obtain. This is not true. Generally, only an application and fee need be submitted, and *presto*—you are one. Usually a bond must also be obtained, which is available from your local insurance agent at a reasonable cost.

A notary public verifies that signatures on documents are genuine and may perform other similar duties as well. For this, a fee is ordinarily charged. Since most contracts, deeds, and other documents of a serious nature need to be notarized, there is constant demand for a notary public's services.

Most businesses that have frequent need for a notary's services like to have one or more employees on their staff be a notary public. Therefore, you may be able to easily tie this in with your current employment. Individuals who need various documents notarized can also use your service.

T-Shirt Lettering: You've seen hundreds, if not thousands, of them—T-shirts adorned with pictures or lettering. Although the term *T-shirt* is used here, this process is by no means limited to T-shirts—sweat shirts, athletic uniforms, jackets, caps, and other garments are all fair game as well.

One of two processes is customarily used to prepare the garments. One is a thermal transfer process whereby transfers (pictures, letters, etc.) are bonded to the garment through a heat process. The other is a silk-screen process whereby the garments are inked through the use of a silk screen. Either process can be used with successful results.

You can prepare garments for individuals, for Little League, and for junior high, high school, college, and adult teams in every athletic event imaginable. Businesses can also be excellent clients, since many of them will buy caps, shirts, or jackets carrying their name, which they will give away or sell at a discount.

Each of the foregoing ideas is described only briefly to give you a general idea of the nature of the activity. If any of them is of interest, you should thoroughly investigate to learn more about the area and to determine the cost of equipment, supplies, facilities, advertising, and all other factors before starting.

Part 5

How to Land a Part-Time Job

I<small>F</small> <small>YOU</small> have decided that you prefer to moonlight by working for someone else, the next step is to go out and land a job. For this, there are certain procedures that can be followed to make the task easier, quicker, and more enjoyable, and which will yield best results. The purpose of this section is to briefly describe those procedures to you.

WHY EMPLOYERS LIKE TO HIRE MOONLIGHTERS

Before making your first contact with a prospective employer, it will be helpful to understand the employer's point of view as it pertains to part-time employees. Just what is the attitude of business owners and managers—do they actually like to hire moonlighters? The answer is unmistakably yes! Some of the reasons are as follows.

1. Passage of the Federal Employee's Part-Time Career Employment Act in 1978 created many part-time federal government jobs and, in effect, gives hiring part-time workers the official "stamp of approval."
2. Often, jobs do not present themselves in neat 8-hour days

for 40-hour weeks. Therefore, it is often ideal to hire a part-timer who will be kept busy full time rather than to hire a full-time employee who will be kept busy only part time.

3. Hiring part-time workers often gives managers more flexibility in arranging work schedules and vacation times.

4. Although many employers pay part-time employees at the same pay rate as full-time workers, a savings can often be obtained in reduced fringe benefit costs in sick leave, paid vacations, and pension plan contributions. Then too, many moonlighters forgo fringe benefits like medical insurance if it is already furnished by their regular employer. In short, it is usually very economical to hire a moonlighter.

5. Many employers have found that moonlighters make excellent employees and approach their work with a great deal of interest and enthusiasm—often more so than regular full-time employees.

6. Many smaller businesses are unable to hire highly skilled professionals or technicians on a full-time basis but can afford their services part time.

7. Since consumers often patronize businesses where a friend, neighbor, relative, or acquaintance works, some employers find that hiring several part-timers instead of one full-time worker increases their number of customers. Also, as any manager of a ladies' clothing store will tell you, the employees are often the store's best customers, and increasing the number of employees through hiring part-timers will result in a direct increase in sales.

8. Hiring someone part time gives the employer a chance to observe the employee on the job before making a commitment to hire the person full time.

This knowledge of employers' attitudes toward hiring moonlighters and of the advantages to employers of doing so can help build your confidence as you start the job-hunting process. It can also provide you with ammunition to use when trying to convince a prospective employer that it makes good business sense to hire you as a part-time employee.

LOCATING A SUITABLE EMPLOYER

As long as you're going to be working anyway, you may as well attempt to find the most ideal part-time job you can. Often, no one method will work best for locating a suitable employer. Therefore, you may need to pursue several or all the job-hunting techniques listed below.

1. Many employment opportunities are never advertised in the newspapers or listed with employment agencies. Rather, these positions are filled quietly with acquaintances of the manager or of the present employees. Therefore, your goal should be to find out about job openings as soon as they develop or maybe even *before* they become available.

The best way to do this is to get the word out. Tell *everyone* you know that you are seeking a part-time job and tell them exactly what type of position would be acceptable. Often, someone will know of an employer who is about to hire a part-time employee or will know of an employee who is about to terminate employment, thus creating an opportunity for you. You can then make direct contact with the employer to inquire about that specific position and may even be able to get an introduction or recommendation from the acquaintance who informed you of the job opening.

You can also attend conventions, seminars, and other business meetings where employers in your line of interest gather. Here is an opportunity to get acquainted with those who do the hiring and to impress them with your interest in their area. Join in discussions and demonstrate your knowledge and ability— and don't hesitate to ask these employers about present or future employment possibilities. Along the same line, you can make personal contacts with employers at country clubs, political rallies, and other places where influential people are apt to congregate.

Another way to locate a job before it is announced to the public is to select a number of employers in your interest area and to contact them personally or through the mail to inquire if they have any openings. On occasion, there will be just such an employer with a recent opening that has not yet been advertised. Since advertising for applicants is costly, and interviewing and screening them is time-consuming, employers might hire you on the spot to save themselves a great deal of time, money, and needless effort.

In using this technique, find out the name of the person who has the final say in hiring employees and contact that person directly rather than contacting the personnel department. That is because the personnel department's function is to screen applicants after an opening becomes available, and you will most likely get lost in the shuffle.

2. Search the help-wanted ads and answer those that sound interesting. Even if you do not seem to possess all the necessary qualifications, apply anyway if you think you can handle the job.

3. Answer any blind ads (those that don't divulge the employer's name) that sound enticing. Often, well-qualified applicants are reluctant to answer these ads since they are fearful that it may be for a high-pressure sales job or similar position. Therefore, if the advertisement is for a legitimate company, your chances of getting the job are increased because the number of applicants may be lower.

4. Consider placing your own advertisement in your local newspaper describing briefly the type of position you are seeking and what you can offer an employer.

5. Register with college, civil service, state, and trade or professional associations' employment agencies. Also consider using a private employment agency, even though a fee must be paid. Often, it is worth paying a fee to land the ideal job, and, in many cases, the employer will pay all or part of it for you.

6. Be observant. If you see construction of a new building or remodeling of a vacant one, it means someone will soon open a business at that site. Ask questions to determine the business's name and make a direct contact.

The length of time required to locate and land the ideal part-time job can vary with many factors. Also, there is no way to predict just when that perfect opportunity will present itself. Therefore, you must steadily apply your job-hunting tactics day after day with great perseverance until you have found the exact moonlighting activity that you want.

APPLYING FOR THE JOB

After you have located a potential moonlighting opportunity, you must next apply for the job. Your goal, of course, is not only to apply for the job but also *get* it.

There is no magical formula that can guarantee that you will get the job that you really want. You can, however, improve your chances immensely by following several tried and tested procedures and by eliminating some commonly made errors that would automatically place you among the also-rans. Some helpful suggestions are as follows:

1. Develop some background knowledge about the company, its products, and its services so that you can intelligently discuss them in a letter of application or personal interview.

2. Demonstrate a genuine interest in the employer's activities and future goals and in your willingness to help achieve those goals.

3. If possible, determine the name of the person who will make the ultimate decision on who will be hired and apply directly to that person by name.

4. Employers are primarily concerned about what you can do for them. Therefore, you should stress how your skill, knowledge, and abilities will be of value to the prospective employer.

5. Have a specific type of job in mind rather than applying for "just anything."

6. Display a positive, winning attitude rather than exhibiting a lackadaisical or negative disposition.

7. Display a friendly, sincere, and businesslike manner in any contact with the prospective employer.

8. Display self-confidence in your ability to do the job without appearing overconfident. Even if you lack confidence on the inside (as is the case with many job applicants), don't let it show on the outside.

9. Do not try to pass yourself off as being able to perform activities that you know you cannot. Rather, state honestly that you are not familiar with that area but are willing to learn.

10. Do not beg or let the employer see how desperately you want or need the job.

In addition to these general guidelines, the following suggestions will be helpful when applying by mail or in person.

Applying by Mail

Whether you send a letter of inquiry or a letter of application, your goal is the same—to arouse the employer's interest in you enough to grant you a personal interview. The following will help you accomplish that goal.

1. Send each prospective employer an individually typed letter that is specifically geared to the position for which you are applying. You can use a standard format for all letters, making necessary changes so that each one is individualized.

2. Enclose a résumé using either the traditional or functional format. With the traditional format, you would list your educational background, experience, and other pertinent factual data. With the functional résumé, you would describe your skills and abilities and explain your specific accomplishments.

3. Type the letter and résumé flawlessly without spelling, typographical, or grammatical errors. Use quality bond paper and a typewriter that produces a good, dark impression. Use an accepted style and proper placement. It should be mentioned

that a high-quality printed or photocopied résumé is usually acceptable.

Fold the letter and résumé according to the accepted business procedure. Use a business-size envelope and follow proper placement and format in typing the address.

The reason for this painstaking attention to detail is that, at this point, the only thing the employer has to judge you by is what you have sent in the mail. If your letter, résumé, or envelope are error-filled and shoddy, the employer will no doubt judge that you are the same way, and your chances for getting an interview, and the job, are gone. Therefore, if you do not have the ability to type a first-class letter and résumé, you should hire someone to do it for you.

Applying in Person

When you reach the point of obtaining a personal interview, you can usually be assured of the fact that you are one of perhaps only two or three finalists for the job. You must now convince the employer that you are the *one* that should be hired. Common sense will be your best guide on how to conduct yourself, as indicated in the following suggestions.

1. Dress appropriately for the type of job for which you are applying. Do not overdress or underdress. Likewise, pay attention to hair, nails, posture, grooming, and other physical attributes.

2. Arrive on time or a few minutes early so you do not keep the employer waiting.

3. If you arrive early, use that time to size up the employer's general philosophy as indicated by decorating, furnishings, and the general attitude of employees. If a company catalog, brochure, or annual report is handy in the reception room, use your time to study it. Besides providing insight into the company, it will provide you with conversational data.

4. Anticipate in advance questions that may be asked of you and give some thought to possible answers.

5. Approach the interview in a relaxed, friendly, and sincere manner.

6. Avoid chewing gum or lighting up to smoke.

7. Stick to discussing the job for which you are applying rather than bringing up inconsequential or potentially controversial topics. Ask carefully thought-out questions to learn about aspects of the job and to demonstrate your general understanding in that area.

8. If the interviewer doesn't ask questions about your skills and abilities and how they will apply to the job, volunteer that information, without making it sound like you are bragging.

9. If the job looks ideal and if you are certain that you can handle it, don't hesitate to tell the employer just that in a sincere and tactful manner.

Follow-up

Directly after your interview, you may wish to write a short letter to the prospective employer. In it you might state that you enjoyed the interview, were impressed by the company, that you have a sincere interest in the job, and that you feel you will be an asset to the company. The purpose of the letter is to remind the employer of you during that critical period when the decision is being made about whom to hire. Your thoughtfulness may be the added touch that gets you the job.

Often, some time may pass without your hearing from the prospective employer after mailing a letter of inquiry or letter of application or after your personal interview. The question that comes to virtually every applicant's mind at this point is, "Should I contact them again?"

Generally, after a proper time period, one follow-up letter expressing your interest in the position will not be looked upon unfavorably by the employer. You should not, however, give the impression that you are trying to rush the employer's decision or that you are trying to exert some type of pressure.

Keep a file of all jobs for which you have applied, indicating dates of letters sent, interviews, and so on. Also, briefly summarize each interview, noting several specific topics that were discussed. This information will provide a good refresher to help you get your bearings if you are called back for another interview or if you want to send a follow-up letter.

NEGOTIATING EMPLOYMENT TERMS

Let's assume that you are now at the point where the employer has just said, "I want to hire you." The next step is to determine exactly what your duties and responsibilities will be, and to agree on other terms of employment, if that was not settled during your interview.

One point that should be emphasized is that the pay rate and amount of fringe benefits are often negotiable. Usually, you have one golden opportunity, and often only one, to negotiate with the employer on an equal basis. That time is *now*, before you agree to accept the job according to the employer's terms.

If you have skills and talents that the employer wants and needs, it is entirely possible that the employer will pay more than initially offered to obtain your services. After you are hired, it is usually difficult to negotiate a pay raise or additional fringe benefits beyond the normal amount that is doled out to all employees as regular pay raises.

Areas that may be negotiable include the pay rate, number of hours to be worked per week or month, schedule of when you are to work, and vacation time. Fringe benefits, including medical, life, optometric, and dental insurance and payment for sick leave, holidays, and vacations may also be negotiable. In general, your goal might be to receive the same pay rate as full-time employees and to receive fringe benefits on a pro rata basis. That means, if you work exactly half the hours of a full-time employee, you would receive half as much paid vacation time, half the pension plan contribution, and so on.

Often, negotiating employment-contract terms amounts to a series of trade-offs. For instance, assume that some factors like pay rate per hour and the number of hours to be worked per week are of greater importance to you than receiving sick leave or paid vacations. To receive the terms you really want, you trade off the ones of lesser importance by accepting decreased benefits or forgoing them altogether.

Whether it is wise to attempt negotiating terms with your employer largely depends upon who is dealing from the strongest position of power—you or the employer. For instance, if the employer is eager to acquire your services and if you have alternative opportunities available to you, you have the power and can probably negotiate very favorable terms. On the other hand, if the employer has several other suitable candidates who can be hired if you turn down the job, and if you want it very much and don't have any other employment possibilities, the employer definitely has the power. No doubt, you would be unable to negotiate terms much different than what the employer offers.

It is therefore necessary for you to make an accurate assessment of your and the employer's relative power positions before you attempt to enter into serious negotiation of employment terms.

After you and the employer have agreed on all terms, you should seek to get the agreement in writing to avoid later misunderstandings and controversies. This becomes increasingly important as the number of specific items in your agreement increases. If it would seem inappropriate or awkward to request that your employer put the terms in writing, at least write the terms down for your own future reference.

JOB SHARING—A NEW CONCEPT

Job sharing is a concept whereby two people share one job. For instance, one person might work mornings and the other would work afternoons. This concept opens up a whole new range of moonlighting opportunities, since two people might apply together for one full-time position and then split it into two part-time jobs.

In order to make the job-sharing concept work, the circumstances must be right. First, the job must be well suited to it. Second, the employer must be convinced that it is a workable and beneficial system. Finally, with many jobs where continuity is required, the two employees must be compatible, and work performance must be consistent from one person to the next.

Often, good communication is the key to making the job-sharing concept work satisfactorily so that each employee knows what the other has done, so no duplication of effort results, so there are no gaps, and so that the work flow continues smoothly.

Quite a number of progressive employers have utilized job sharing with the same satisfactory results experienced by other employers who hire moonlighters. An outstanding advantage to the employer is that the job-sharing employees accept full responsibility for someone to always be on the job. Therefore, if one person is ill or on vacation, the other will be on duty, and there is never a slowdown in productivity.

Part 6

How to Establish Your Own Business or Service

Even though you will be operating your own business or service on a part-time basis, your customers will expect you to provide the same type of first-rate service available from any full-time operation. Therefore, it is necessary for you to organize and operate your business or service according to well-established, tried, and tested business principles and practices.

This section identifies areas that require your attention and briefly describes some of the major factors you should consider. This information, along with your own study and investigation, will help you to establish your operation on a solid basis and ensure that it will continue efficiently and successfully.

ORGANIZING YOUR BUSINESS OR SERVICE

The most important step in organizing your business or service can be summarized in one word—*planning*. This activity takes time, but it will pay big dividends by saving money and time, and yes, headaches, in the future.

Developing an Image

Each business or service operation should be developed with a "look," or image, of its own. This image is the appearance or impression that you project to others. That is, do you handle high-, medium-, or low-quality goods? Do your offerings appeal mostly to the rich, the poor, or the middle class? Do you offer something for everyone or are you highly specialized?

Any image is fine—as long as it is consistently displayed and followed in all that you do. The image you are trying to create will largely set the tone for all your business activities, including selection of a location, type of merchandise handled, quality of furnishings and fixtures installed, prices charged, and so on.

Choosing Your Form of Business Ownership

Your business or service can be organized as a *sole proprietorship, partnership,* or *corporation.* Primarily, these designations are legal in nature and do not affect how you would actually operate. The number of people involved largely dictates the form of organization to select.

Most people who operate a part-time business or service initially organize it as a sole proprietorship if the operation is owned by only one person. The advantage of doing so is that it is simple to establish by merely selecting a name and perhaps registering it with the county recorder. Also, there is virtually no cost or legal procedures involved. The primary disadvantage is that you are personally responsible for all debts incurred by the business, should your operation become a failure.

If two or more people join together, the partnership form of organization can be used. A written agreement should be drawn, before you begin operations. This should state the duties, rights, responsibilities, and financial contributions of all parties. It should also provide a statement of how profits and losses are to be divided and outline a procedure to be followed if a partner wishes to withdraw from the operation.

An advantage of the partnership form of ownership is that there are more people to contribute ideas, money, and labor, and to share potential losses. Major disadvantages are that the profits are divided among more people and that each partner is fully responsible for the total debts of the partnership should it fail. Another possible disadvantage, which should not be taken lightly, is that it is often difficult for two or more people to work together closely without problems and controversies arising.

In most states, a corporation can be formed by as few as one or two people. One advantage is that your financial responsibility is limited to your investment in the business should your operation fail or be sued. Also, if your income is high, there may be a tax advantage.

A disadvantage of the corporate form of ownership is that it is practically necessary to use the services of a lawyer to complete the incorporation procedures and the cost is therefore high—usually several hundred dollars. Also, there are more requirements that must be met for filing annual state reports, paying fees, recording minutes of annual meetings, and so on.

Planning Your Finances

One of the prime reasons for business failure is that of starting out *undercapitalized*—that is, with too little money. Therefore, before starting, you should make a list of every cost that will be required to establish your operation so you will know how much money will be needed.

Include the cost of equipment, vehicles, fixtures, office supplies, sales supplies, telephone and utility hookups and deposits, licenses, permits, and insurance. Also include legal and professional fees, printing costs for business cards, price lists, etcetera, beginning merchandise inventory, and initial advertising costs. In addition, any costs for renting or buying a business location and for remodeling and redecorating must be included.

The next step should be to develop a budget that lists all expected costs and expenses. Your budget can cover any time period, but a month is usually ideal. Include all expenditures that you are likely to incur in your budget period and also prorate those items that are paid unevenly throughout the year. For instance, assume that you have a $240 insurance premium that is paid once per year. If you develop a monthly budget, it should include one-twelfth of that annual insurance premium, or $20.

Items that should be built into your budget include the cost of materials or ingredients, rent, supplies, advertising, telephone charges, utilities, loan payments, insurance, postage and freight charges, vehicle expenses, and salaries paid to employees. Also, include costs for licenses and permits, taxes, and legal, accounting, or professional fees. Since it is impossible to anticipate all costs and expenses, an amount of perhaps 5 to 10 percent of the total budget should be added for miscellaneous expenses.

You have now identified the amount of money you will need to get started. The next step is to "find" the money. The easiest source is to use funds you already have. If you do not have sufficient money on hand or do not want to use that money, you must find other sources. These might include borrowing the cash value of a permanent life insurance policy or borrowing from a bank, credit union, friend, or relative. Another solution is to include one or more partners.

Selecting a Location

For many types of business operations, the most important ingredient that will lead to success or failure can be described in one word—*location*. What constitutes a good location will vary with the type of business or service. In general, though, it means being highly visible in a high traffic area and being well situated for your potential customers. In many cases, the ideal location may be unavailable or the cost may be prohibitive. Therefore, you must select the best location you can find, which is within your price range.

Many part-time businesses and service operations can be most logically operated from your own home. In those situations, strong advertising and promotion may be necessary to make potential customers aware of your offerings.

When selecting a location, whether it is in a business district or in your home, you must make yourself aware of city and county *zoning ordinances.* These are regulations which specify that each parcel of property in the community can be used for specific purposes only. If your proposed location is not zoned for your intended use, it is possible to appeal to the zoning commission to obtain a *zoning variance.* If granted, this will allow you to use the property for the purpose you have in mind.

Locating Suppliers

If your business or service involves the sale of products or the use of replacement parts, you will need to locate suppliers of those goods. In some cases, you will need to buy through distributors or wholesalers, while at other times it may be possible to buy directly from manufacturers.

Some suppliers can be located by checking the yellow pages of a city telephone directory; look under your product's subject classification. Others might be located by obtaining a name and address from a product label or container and by then writing or telephoning the company. You can get the telephone number by calling directory assistance in that area code, or you might call WATS-line directory assistance, 1-800-555-1212, for a toll-free number to dial.

Guide to Associations, available at most university and public libraries, can be checked for names of associations in your product area. You can then contact these associations, and they can most likely put you in touch with some of their members who will be able to supply what you need. Similarly, you can obtain names and addresses of manufacturers from the *Thomas Register of Manufacturers,* which is available in most well-stocked libraries.

Other people dealing in your same type of business or service can also be good contacts, since they may recommend the suppliers from whom they obtain merchandise and replacement parts. No doubt, you will need to contact someone outside your immediate trade area, since it would be presumptuous to expect a competitor to help you get started.

Securing Licenses and Permits

City, county, state, and/or federal licenses or permits are often required before entering a particular business or service operation. Often, these are issued solely as a fund-raising measure, and they are therefore easy to obtain by simply submitting a fee.

In other cases, licensing is used as a method of regulating the competency of those entering a particular field and to protect the public from unknowledgeable operators. Often, an exam is administered, and moral and financial requirements may need to be met as well.

Check with the proper officials, or your attorney, to determine what licenses and permits are needed, since offering your services without proper authorization can result in severe penalties, and you may be forced to discontinue operations.

Many states, and some cities and counties, require that sales taxes be collected. The state sales tax permit is available from the State Department of Revenue. City and county permits are available from the tax department in those jurisdictions.

Even though a certain amount of "red tape" must be waded through to obtain some licenses and permits, this is usually a once-in-a-business-lifetime occurence. After that, it is usually a matter of simply submitting an annual renewal fee. In some cases, however, annual continuing-education requirements must be met for license renewal.

Using Professional Services

It is extremely difficult, perhaps impossible, for any one person to be an expert in every phase of operating a business. Therefore, it sometimes becomes necessary to rely upon the professional services of others.

If you have legal questions, consult an attorney. If you do not understand bookkeeping, accounting, or income tax preparation, call in an accountant. If you are struggling with some other phase of business operations, you might utilize the services of a business consultant. A source of free advice is the Service Corps of Retired Executives. This service, called SCORE, is made available by the Small Business Administration and provides assistance for businesses of all sizes. Contact your local SBA office if this service sounds of interest to you.

Professional organizations and associations are also a good source of information. You can often learn a great deal from their newsletters, magazines, and conventions. Check your library's *Guide to Associations* for a list of those in your area of interest.

OPERATING YOUR BUSINESS OR SERVICE

There is generally no one right way in which to operate a business or service, but there are dozens of wrong ways. Often, development of the proper business attitude in a few key areas, like those discussed below, can be very helpful to get your operation started the "right" way.

Defining the Scope of Your Operations

Take out a sheet of paper and write down the answers to these questions:

    1. Exactly what product or service do you propose to offer?

    2. Upon what basis will you price your merchandise or services?

    3. What type of warranty or guarantee will you extend to buyers of your goods or services?

4. What days or nights will you be open for business?

5. If several people are involved, who is in charge of what?

6. What is the procedure that will be followed for making decisions?

7. What procedures will you follow for granting refunds or exchanges?

8. What is your policy for granting credit?

9. What is your policy pertaining to taking personal checks from customers?

10. At what price can friends, relatives, and employees purchase your goods and services?

11. What is your policy for handling shoplifters?

12. How often, and when, will your bookkeeping be done, and who will do it?

13. What are your plans for future expansion?

You have now quite clearly defined the scope of your operations—that is, what you are going to do and how you are going to do it. Keep your written answers handy, where you can refer to them often. They will provide the basis for consistency in your dealings with your customers and in your own internal activities.

Identifying Your Customers

Who are your customers? Your initial reaction might be, "I can sell to anyone." Perhaps this is true, but many products and services are not used by everyone; they are used by a certain select type of customer with specific interests or needs in that area.

Therefore, in order to direct your advertising to the most fruitful prospects and to provide the type of product or service that your customers expect, it is necessary to identify as closely as possible who your potential customers really are. This does not mean that you will identify them by name. What you will identify are common *characteristics* that your customers are most likely to possess. This is called developing a *buyer profile*.

To develop a buyer profile for your product or service, write down characteristics that a typical customer might possess in the following categories.

1. Age
2. Sex
3. Income
4. Marital status
5. Family size
6. Physical characteristics
7. Occupation
8. Hobbies
9. Social activities
10. Club memberships, etcetera
11. Social status
12. Ownership of certain items
13. Geographic location
14. Personal goals
15. Professional goals

Although buyers of your product or service do not all match the same mold, they probably share enough common traits to give you some direction to follow in many of your business activities. Specifically, you should match your offerings to those customers who are most likely to use them.

Advertising and Promoting Your Offerings

Often, a business or service that is not advertised and promoted is one of the best-kept secrets in town. If you want prospective customers to know about your offerings, you must tell them—and more than once. The constant blitz of advertising by already world-famous soft drink manufacturers is proof of that.

The advertising and promotional techniques that are appropriate for your goods and services will vary with many factors. These include your advertising budget, your location, your customers' special interests, and the type of goods or services you offer.

The followiing list presents many promotional ideas. Often,

no one single technique will produce satisfactory results, and a promotional program must be devised that creates a "mix" of activities.

1. Advertise in newspapers, radio, and television.

2. Advertise in special-interest magazines or newsletters that are read by prospective customers for your goods and services.

3. Place an advertisement in the yellow pages of your telephone directory.

4. If you can identify prospects by name, use direct mail.

5. Telephone the prospects you can identify by name, or simply call every name in the directory or those selected at random.

6. Post flyers on community-service and college campus bulletin boards.

7. If your operation is unique, approach a newspaper, radio station, or television station about their interest in doing a feature story on your activities.

8. Have T-shirts, jackets, or caps printed with your business name on them and sell them at a discount or give them away.

9. Give away advertising specialties like matchbooks, pens, or calendars with your name on them.

10. Have business cards printed and distribute them to everyone you meet.

11. Join clubs and organizations and, in general, become more visible. Tell everyone, subtly, about your business or service.

12. Sponsor an adult or Little League team in baseball, bowling, softball, or some other activity.

13. Place a large, highly visible sign at your business location.

14. Ask every satisfied customer to spread the word.

15. Have your business name painted on your vehicle or use pressure-sensitive signs.

16. Have bumper stickers printed for your own vehicle and for others as well.

17. Develop a working relationship with others who provide complementary goods and services, whereby you refer customers to each other.

18. Give free samples, or huge discounts, to introduce prospects to your offerings.

19. Have business checks and stationery printed with your business name on them.

20. Make cold calls, going door to door in search of someone who can use your goods or services.

For best results, you should develop a program, whereby each advertisement and promotional activity is designed with a specific purpose in mind, rather than using a haphazard, "shotgun" approach of advertising whenever the whim hits you. In some cases, this program might consist of heavy advertising during your *season*, with little or no advertising the rest of the year. In others, you might concentrate your budget to provide a burst of advertising periodically throughout the year. For many, steady advertising year round will bring the best results.

Part 7

How to Perform as a Salesperson

Two factors that will play a major role in determining your success as a salesperson are your selection of a product or service to sell and your ability to properly apply basic sales techniques.

SELECTING A PRODUCT OR SERVICE TO SELL

Dozens, or perhaps even hundreds, of products and services are well suited to being sold on a part-time basis. Each of them has its own characteristics as far as income potential and application of sales procedures.

With some, such as real estate and life insurance, relatively few sales are made, but the profit potential from each sale is great. With others, like cosmetics or household products, the income per sale may be rather low, but many sales are usually generated. Some products, like investment securities, are intangible, while others, like sewing machines, are tangible. Potential for frequent repeat sales exists for some products, such as food supplements, whereas others, like vacuum cleaners or houses, are ordinarily purchased only a few times in a lifetime.

Much training and background knowledge is required to become qualified to sell in some areas, while very little, if any, is necessary for others. In some cases, special licensing and certification is necessary, whereas no such requirements exist in many other cases. Some products and services can be used by virtually everyone, while others appeal mainly to persons of a certain age, sex, income level, or special interest.

Highly polished sales techniques are necessary to be successful in selling some products or services, while hard work, perseverance, and a basic ability to sell are the main prerequisites for others. Sales presentations for some products or services might last for hours, while others will be conducted in only a few minutes. In some cases, prospects are eager to own what you are selling, but in others, you must convince them that they need the item. Some sales areas must be pursued rather steadily to become successful, while others can be approached on a sporadic basis.

The list of differences that exist in selling various products and services could continue, but you no doubt get the basic idea. That is, regardless of your sales abilities, time availability, personality, and personal interests, there will be several sales areas for which you will be well suited. Before you select a product or service to sell, therefore, you should investigate every aspect of it and of the sales techniques and procedures that will be involved.

Perhaps the most important factor of all is that you select a product or service in which you truly believe. You must possess a firm conviction that what you are selling is of great value and benefit to your customers. Without this belief, you will find it extremely difficult to be very convincing while making your sales presentation.

Another important aspect of your selection process is to choose a company whose reputation, methods, goals, sales assistance, and payment rate are acceptable to you. Since there are usually a number of companies offering similar products and services, you should investigate what each one has to offer you before becoming affiliated with one of them.

APPLYING SALES TECHNIQUES

Although many differences exist from one product or service to another, the same basic sales techniques can be universally applied. Therefore, if you become successful in selling one type of item, you can most likely carry that success over to selling many other types of products or services as well.

Mastery of the sales techniques that are briefly described below should help you become successful in virtually any area of sales.

Identifying and Fulfilling the Prospect's Needs

This area, identifying and fulfilling the prospect's needs, is the essence of salesmanship. You must determine the prospect's underlying needs and then show how your product or service will satisfy those needs.

This is not an easy task, since prospective buyers often do not divulge their innermost thoughts. In many cases, they are not even aware of their own reasons for buying or not buying. Using tactful questions will help you gather information. Then, you must analyze that data and interpret for the prospects how your offerings can be of benefit to them.

Keep firmly in mind that it is always the benefits or satisfactions that will be received that are of utmost interest to a buyer.

Prospecting for Customers

Your ability to prospect for customers will most likely determine your success or failure as a salesperson more than any other sales technique. Without prospecting—that is, locating potential customers who have a need for your product or service and who can afford it—you will have very few customers to whom your sales presentation can be made.

The prospecting techniques that work best will vary with the type of product or service being sold. Usually, several of the techniques shown below need to be used to develop a successful prospecting program.

1. Each time you make a sales presentation, ask if that prospect can recommend others whom you can contact by name.

2. Gather names from your local newspaper and telephone them or call on them in person. The newly engaged or married, the recently promoted, and new parents have all had a major change in their lives that indicates they now have a need for a whole range of goods and services.

3. Join groups, clubs, and organizations to enlarge your circle of acquaintances. Tell everyone with whom you come in contact about your goods and services.

4. Make cold calls. That is, telephone names selected at random from the telephone directory or make personal visits to every home in a section of the community.

5. Be observant. Look for situations where someone can use your offerings.

6. Enlist the services of "bird dogs." These are people who actively keep their eyes and ears open to locate prospects for you.

7. Develop a working relationship with other salespeople or business operators whereby you refer customers to each other.

8. Have business cards printed and distribute them at every opportunity.

9. Don't overlook friends, relatives, co-workers, and others whom you know. If you truly believe in what you are selling, you will be doing them a favor by giving them a chance to buy from you.

10. Keep in touch with present and former customers, since they will most likely buy a similar product or service again sometime in the future.

Prospecting for customers is an ongoing process that should be worked at continually. If you steadily work at each of the prospecting techniques suggested here, each may yield one or two good names per week or per month and you will never have to worry about having potential customers for your goods and services.

Preparing a Professional Sales Presentation

It is foolish to attempt selling your product or service without the use of a planned sales presentation.

Your planned sales presentation should include the topics you want to cover and the most logical order in which they should be presented. You might develop a *canned presentation,* where every word is memorized, or you can use a *sales-presentation outline,* where major topics and subtopics are committed to memory.

The canned presentation works well where you call on each prospect only once or very infrequently. Its advantages are that the presentation is complete, well organized, and efficient. Its disadvantages are that it can become boring to use time after time, is inflexible, may sound memorized, and it may be difficult to get back on track if the prospect interrupts your sales story.

The sales-presentation outline can be used effectively for selling any product or service. It provides the advantages of planning, completeness, flexibility, and the ability to deliver a completely natural–sounding presentation. Its only disadvantage might be that since the topics to be covered are memorized, you could forget one and leave out an important point.

Regardless of the sales-presentation method used, the important factor is that you give a good deal of advance thought to what you will say and how you can most effectively say it.

In addition to the verbal presentation, you should also develop a *demonstration* that appeals to the prospect's sense of sight, smell, taste, touch, or hearing. Your demonstration should be coordinated with your verbal statements to provide a smooth-flowing presentation that appeals to more than one of your prospect's senses at the same time.

Making the Sales Presentation

In most cases, if you have done an effective job of prospecting, you are now standing face to face with someone who needs your product or service, can afford it, and should buy it. Now you must convince your prospect of that.

Many factors are involved in making an effective sales presentation. Primarily, though, it amounts to selecting the right approach. Since different people buy the same product or service for different reasons, you must determine each prospect's strongest buying motives and direct your presentation to fit those interests.

Keep your presentation on a friendly, conversational level that is aggressive but not high pressure. Involve the prospect by asking periodic questions and by having the person participate in your demonstration. Make certain that each concept you present is clearly understood by your prospect and get agreement on each point before moving on to the next one. Move along at a lively pace that is in step with your prospect's comprehension level.

Inconsequential topics like the weather and potentially volatile ones like politics or religion should be avoided. Stick strictly to business. Your prospects will appreciate your consideration of their time, and you will be able to make efficient use of yours as well.

Overcoming Objections

You can expect your prospects to raise one or more objections before they give in and say, "Yes, I will buy." Some raise objections out of sheer habit, others feel it is their duty, and others don't want to look like a pushover. Then, there are some with legitimate questions and concerns.

What should your attitude be toward the prospect's objections? Well, first of all, you should *expect* that they will be raised. Secondly, you should actually *welcome* them, since it shows you the prospect's line of thinking and divulges the reasons why the prospect has not yet bought. Then, after disposing of the objection, you will be one step closer to completing the sale.

One of the most difficult tasks in sales is to differentiate between bona fide objections on the one hand and excuses on the other. The difference is that an objection is a legitimate, sincere concern, whereas an excuse is an insincere or contrived reason. Tactful questioning and your own observation of the prospect's needs and wants can help you distinguish whether the resistance is sincere or not.

Once you have been able to classify the prospect's resistance as an excuse rather than a legitimate objection, you must prod and probe to locate the prospect's real reason for not buying. When you have done that, you can then eliminate the objection and wrap up the sale.

Objections can be handled in a number of ways, including the following:

1. Ignore it. If it is of minor consequence, the prospect will forget it, and you will not hear the objection again. If it is of great importance, the prospect will raise it again, and you can handle it then.

2. Turn the prospect's reason for not buying into the very reason why they should buy. For instance, if the prospect is reluctant to buy an investment security because of inability to afford it, that may be exactly why they should buy—to start accumulating some money.

3. Answer the objection head on and dispose of it once and for always.

4. Demonstrate the product to prove what you say is true.

5. Show case histories of how others have benefited from using your product or service.

6. Ask the prospect a series of leading questions and let the person dispose of his or her own objection through their own answers.

7. Let prospects talk themselves out until they get whatever is bothering them off their chest.

8. Make a firm and point-blank denial of your prospect's accusation about your product, service, or company if it is not true.

9. Appeal to your prospect's sense of duty, responsibility, maturity, or logic.

10. If all else fails, ask your prospect to level with you and divulge the real reason for refusal to buy.

Your prospect will not always volunteer, "Yes, I agree, you are right," after you have answered an objection. Therefore, you may need to use a question like, "Don't you agree?" or "That won't present a problem for you after all, will it?" to verify that the prospect's objection has been overcome.

Closing the Sale

Many prospects agree that they need the product or service, want it, can make beneficial use of it, and can afford it. Yet, they fail to make the purchase. Therefore, you earn nothing for all of your fine prospecting and sales-presentation efforts.

A common trait shared by virtually all successful salespeople is that they are strong closers—they can get the prospect to sign on the dotted line. Often, the key to this is perseverance. You should not fold up your act and meekly shuffle out the door just because the prospect said no. Instead, you should hang in there to complete the job you started. You may need to ask the prospect again and again and again before you finally make the sale or resign yourself to the fact that you never will—at least not right now.

You should use indirect methods of asking your prospect to buy rather than a direct question like, "Do you want to buy it?" This technique uses leading questions such as the following: "Do you prefer the green one or the blue one?" "Your husband will sure appreciate this, won't he?" "Isn't this the prettiest one you've ever seen?" "How much of a down payment would be comfortable?" "Did you ever imagine you would have a chance to actually own anything this nice?"

If your prospect gives a positive or leading response to your question, proceed immediately to closing the deal by starting to fill out the order form, boxing up the merchandise, or by making some other forceful and positive gesture that indicates that you assume the prospect has made the purchase. You must be careful, of course, so that you do not appear too presumptuous or become overbearing and pushy.

If the prospect stops you or has failed to give a positive response, review some of the benefits that the prospect will receive from making the purchase and try to close the sale again. Keep following this procedure until the sale is made or until good judgment tells you that it is time to terminate the presentation. At that point, take steps to retain the prospect's goodwill so you will be in a position to make a follow-up call later on.

It should be pointed out that not all prospects become buyers regardless of how great a job you have done in prospecting and making the sales presentation. Therefore, when you come to recognize that you are not going to make the sale to a particular prospect, move on to someone else who holds better potential for you.

Follow-up

Many prospects do not buy the first time they are contacted, or maybe even the second or the third time. Eventually, though, many of them will become buyers.

You should therefore develop a filing system where you catalog prospects, indicating when they should next be contacted. Indicate on your file card any prospect information that will be useful to you in the future, such as the person's strongest interests or needs.

Keep in contact with prospects via the telephone, direct mail, or in person to "keep them warm." Try to deliver some new information or do something of service for your prospects each time you contact them. Also, keep in contact with present customers, since many of them will buy a similar product or service in the future.

The amount of time and effort that should be devoted to follow-up and to other sales activities depends largely upon the nature of what you are selling. If you make relatively few sales but each is a high-ticket item, every prospect will be of great value to you and will merit much time and attention. On the other hand, if you sell low-priced items to a large number of customers, you should not devote an undue amount of time pursuing a few hard-to-get prospects.

After a sale is made, you should follow up to see that the product was delivered, that the prospect understands how to use it, and that the prospect is fully satisfied. Often, just a telephone call is sufficient. This provides a great opportunity to cement a lasting business relationship with your new customer.

Managing Your Time

One of the great advantages of being a salesperson is that you can often work when you want, without any set time schedule. This can also be one of the biggest disadvantages for those who find it easy to put things off until later.

You can improve your utilization of time by following a few simple suggestions, as listed below:

1. Work during the hours of the day or night when most can be accomplished. For instance, if your prospects are easiest

to reach at a certain time, work then rather than when they are more difficult to locate.

2. Plan a full week's work in advance, indicating on a calendar or schedule exactly when you plan to work.

3. Each night, plan the following day's activities, indicating exactly what you will do, who you will see, and so on.

4. Make appointments, if practical, to conserve time.

5. Use the telephone whenever possible, instead of making time-consuming personal visits.

6. Schedule your driving activities so that the shortest and most efficient route is traveled.

7. Devote your designated work hours strictly to business rather than also performing personal errands during that time.

8. When dealing with customers, confine your conversation to business only, instead of wasting time on small talk.

9. Become an expert at spotting high-quality prospects so that your time can be devoted to working with those who will most likely become buyers.

10. Perform paper work, research, and other nonselling activities during times other than regular selling hours.

As a well-prepared salesperson, you will accomplish much more in less time and with less effort. Always be alert to ways you can conserve time, without cutting corners, for it will pay big dividends by increasing both your productivity and your income.

Part 8

Getting Started

Now you know what moonlighting is all about. It is a great way to earn that extra money for a real vacation, your dream house, a new car, or to start a real savings and investment program. It can be the opportunity to put some real challenge and excitement into your life. Perhaps it is the way to ease into a new career that will change your life.

Regardless of the appeal that moonlighting holds for you, there is one thing that must be done before you will realize your goal. You must *get started*. Choose a moonlighting area that appeals to you, investigate it thoroughly, and take one step, and then another, and soon you too will realize the rewards of moonlighting!

Index